8TH GRADE
READING COMPREHENSION
SUCCESS

LEARNINGEXPRESS SKILL BUILDERS

8TH GRADE READING COMPREHENSION SUCCESS

Elizabeth Chesla

LEARNINGEXPRESS

NEW YORK

Printed in the United States of America

9 8 7 6 5 4 3 2 1

First Edition

ISBN 1-57685-391-8

For more information or to place an order, contact LearningExpress at:

900 Broadway

Suite 604

New York, NY 10003

Or visit us at:

www.learnatest.com

An Important Note to
Our Library Readers

CONTENTS

HOW TO USE THIS BOOK

Eighth grade is an exciting year full of changes and challenges. It's also an important year academically. As an eighth grader, you'll be required to take tests that measure your reading, writing, and math skills. This year is also your last chance to brush up your academic skills before high school. And because you'll need to read for almost all of your classes, reading comprehension is perhaps the most important set of skills you'll need to succeed.

In eighth grade and beyond, you'll be asked to read, understand, and interpret a variety of texts, including stories and poems, reports, essays, and scientific and technical information. While a lot of your learning will still take place in the classroom, you'll be expected to read more and more information on your own, outside class. You'll need not only to understand what you read but also to respond to and assess what you read. And as the texts you read become more complex, you'll spend a lot more time "reading between the lines" and drawing your own conclusions from the text.

As you work through the lessons in this book you will build your critical reading and thinking skills. Each of the 20 short lessons should take about a half hour to complete. You'll start with the basics and move into more complex reading strategies. While each chapter can be an effective skill builder on its own, it is important that you proceed through this book in order, from Lesson 1 through Lesson 20. Each lesson builds on skills and ideas discussed in the previous chapters, and as you move through this book and your reading comprehension skills improve, the practice passages will become longer and more difficult.

The lessons are divided into four sections. Each section focuses on a different group of related reading comprehension strategies. These strategies are outlined at the beginning of each section and reviewed at the end of the section in a special Putting It All Together lesson.

Each lesson includes several exercises for you to practice the skills you have learned. To be sure you're on the right track, at the end of each lesson you'll find answers and explanations for the practice questions. You'll also find a section called Skill Building until Next Time after each practice session. These are helpful suggestions for practicing your new skills.

This book also includes a pretest and post-test. To help you measure your progress, do the Pretest before you begin Lesson 1. The Pretest will give you a sense of your strengths and weaknesses so you can focus on specific chapters. After you finish the lessons, take the Post-test. You'll be able to see how much your reading comprehension skills have improved. You'll also be able to find out if there are areas in which you may still need practice.

PRETEST

Before you begin, find out how much you already know about reading comprehension—and how much you need to learn. Take this pretest. These 40 multiple-choice questions cover all of the topics in this book. If your score is high, you might move through this book more quickly than you expected. If your score is low, you may need more than 30 minutes to get through each lesson.

On the following page there is an answer sheet, or you can just circle the correct answers. If you don't own this book, write the numbers 1–40 on a sheet of paper, and write your answers next to the numbers. Take as much time as you need for this test. Then use the answer key at the end of the test to check your answers. The key tells you which lesson covers the strategy in that question.

Good luck!

1.	ⓐ	ⓑ	ⓒ	ⓓ
2.	ⓐ	ⓑ	ⓒ	ⓓ
3.	ⓐ	ⓑ	ⓒ	ⓓ
4.	ⓐ	ⓑ	ⓒ	ⓓ
5.	ⓐ	ⓑ	ⓒ	ⓓ
6.	ⓐ	ⓑ	ⓒ	ⓓ
7.	ⓐ	ⓑ	ⓒ	ⓓ
8.	ⓐ	ⓑ	ⓒ	ⓓ
9.	ⓐ	ⓑ	ⓒ	ⓓ
10.	ⓐ	ⓑ	ⓒ	ⓓ
11.	ⓐ	ⓑ	ⓒ	ⓓ
12.	ⓐ	ⓑ	ⓒ	ⓓ
13.	ⓐ	ⓑ	ⓒ	ⓓ
14.	ⓐ	ⓑ	ⓒ	ⓓ
15.	ⓐ	ⓑ	ⓒ	ⓓ

16.	ⓐ	ⓑ	ⓒ	ⓓ
17.	ⓐ	ⓑ	ⓒ	ⓓ
18.	ⓐ	ⓑ	ⓒ	ⓓ
19.	ⓐ	ⓑ	ⓒ	ⓓ
20.	ⓐ	ⓑ	ⓒ	ⓓ
21.	ⓐ	ⓑ	ⓒ	ⓓ
22.	ⓐ	ⓑ	ⓒ	ⓓ
23.	ⓐ	ⓑ	ⓒ	ⓓ
24.	ⓐ	ⓑ	ⓒ	ⓓ
25.	ⓐ	ⓑ	ⓒ	ⓓ
26.	ⓐ	ⓑ	ⓒ	ⓓ
27.	ⓐ	ⓑ	ⓒ	ⓓ
28.	ⓐ	ⓑ	ⓒ	ⓓ
29.	ⓐ	ⓑ	ⓒ	ⓓ
30.	ⓐ	ⓑ	ⓒ	ⓓ

31.	ⓐ	ⓑ	ⓒ	ⓓ
32.	ⓐ	ⓑ	ⓒ	ⓓ
33.	ⓐ	ⓑ	ⓒ	ⓓ
34.	ⓐ	ⓑ	ⓒ	ⓓ
35.	ⓐ	ⓑ	ⓒ	ⓓ
36.	ⓐ	ⓑ	ⓒ	ⓓ
37.	ⓐ	ⓑ	ⓒ	ⓓ
38.	ⓐ	ⓑ	ⓒ	ⓓ
39.	ⓐ	ⓑ	ⓒ	ⓓ
40.	ⓐ	ⓑ	ⓒ	ⓓ

Directions: Read each passage below carefully and actively. Answer the questions that follow each passage.

ECOSYSTEMS

An ecosystem is a group of animals and plants living in a specific region and interacting with one another and with their physical environment. Ecosystems include physical and chemical components, such as soils, water, and nutrients. These components support the organisms living in the ecosystem.

Ecosystems can also be thought of as the interactions among all organisms in a given habitat. These organisms may range from large animals to microscopic bacteria and work together in various ways. For example, one species may serve as food for another.

People are part of the ecosystems where they live and work. Human activities, such as housing developments and trash disposal, can greatly harm or even destroy local ecosystems. Proper ecosystem management is crucial for the overall health and diversity of our planet. We must find ways to protect local ecosystems without stifling economic development.

QUESTIONS

1. Which sentence best expresses the main idea of this passage?
   a. Our actions can have a great impact on our ecosystems.
   b. Ecosystems have been badly managed in the past.
   c. Humans must clean up their trash.
   d. Ecosystems interact with one another.

2. Which of the following best sums up the activities within an ecosystem?
   a. predator–prey relationships
   b. interactions among all members
   c. human–animal interactions
   d. human relationship with the environment

3. An ecosystem can most accurately be defined as
   a. a specific place.
   b. a community of plants and animals.
   c. a group of animals working together.
   d. a protected environment.

THE STORY OF DR. MUDD

On the night of April 14, 1865—five days after the Civil War ended—President Abraham Lincoln was attending the theater in Washington, D.C. In the middle of the performance, an actor named John Wilkes Booth, seeking to avenge the defeat of the South, slipped into the presidential box and shot the President.

Booth escaped the theater but broke his leg when he leaped from the President's box seat to the stage. Before anybody could stop him, he limped out the back door, mounted a waiting horse, and disappeared into the night with a fellow conspirator.

Five hours later, at four o'clock in the morning, Booth and his companion knocked on the door of Samuel Mudd, a doctor living in southern Maryland. Dr. Mudd knew nothing about the assassination of the President, and acting as any doctor would to a stranger in distress, set the leg and persuaded the two travelers to stay in his house for the rest of the night. The next morning, Booth and his friend, using false names, paid the bill and departed.

Because of this merciful act, Dr. Mudd was arrested, taken to Washington, and tried on the charge that he was a friend of Booth's and therefore helped plan the assassination.

Dr. Mudd insisted that he knew nothing of the plot. But the military courts, angry at the President's death, sentenced the unfortunate doctor to life imprisonment. Dr. Mudd was imprisoned at Fort Jefferson, an island fortress in the middle of the sea about 120 miles west of the southern tip of Florida.

As horrible and unjust as this punishment must have been, a greater plight lurked at Fort Jefferson. The warm, humid climate was a perfect breeding ground for mosquitoes. Again and again, these pests spread yellow fever germs to prisoners and guards alike.

When the fever struck, Dr. Mudd volunteered his services, because he was the only doctor on the island. He had to fight the disease, even after he was infected himself. In spite of the fact that the guards and other inmates called him "that Lincoln murderer," and treated him very badly, he worked hard to fight the disease.

Meanwhile, his wife was working heroically back in Washington for her husband's cause. After a four-year struggle, she secured a pardon for him—for a crime he never committed.

Dr. Mudd returned to Maryland to pick up the pieces of his shattered life. Soon after Dr. Mudd's release, Fort Jefferson was abandoned. Today, the one-time prison sits in ruins, inhabited only by birds—and mosquitoes.

QUESTIONS

4. Dr. Mudd was convicted because
   a. he helped Booth assassinate Lincoln.
   b. he helped Booth get away.
   c. the military courts wanted someone to pay for Lincoln's death.
   d. he lied to the military courts.

5. An alternative title for this passage might be
   a. Lincoln's Assassination.
   b. Good Doc Gone Bad.
   c. A Prison Abandoned.
   d. An Unfair Trial for a Fair Man.

6. What sort of doctor was Dr. Mudd?

    a. careless, sloppy

    b. generous, caring

    c. greedy, money-hungry

    d. cold-hearted, unfeeling

7. Dr. Mudd fought the yellow fever outbreak at Fort Jefferson because

    a. there was no one else to treat the sick prisoners.

    b. he thought it would help get him a pardon.

    c. he didn't want to get sick himself.

    d. he was forced to by the prison warden.

8. Read this sentence from the essay.

As horrible and unjust as this punishment must have been, a greater <u>plight</u> lurked at Fort Jefferson.

As it is used in this passage, *plight* most nearly means

    a. challenge.

    b. difficulty.

    c. scare.

    d. sickness.

YEAR-ROUND SCHOOL VS. REGULAR SCHOOL SCHEDULE

Both year-round school and regular school schedules are found throughout the United States. With year-round school schedules, students attend classes for nine weeks, and then have three weeks' vacation. This continues all year long. The regular school schedule requires that students attend classes from September to June, with a three-month summer vacation at the end of the year. This schedule began because farmers needed their children at home to help with crops during the summer. Today, most people work in businesses and offices. Year-round school is easier for parents who work in businesses and don't have the summer to be with their children. The regular school schedule is great for kids who like to have a long summer vacation. While some educational systems have changed their schedules to keep up with their population, others still use the old agrarian calendar. Both systems have disadvantages and advantages, which is why schools use different systems.

QUESTIONS

9. Which of the following statements from the passage represents the author's **opinion**?

    a. Year-round school is easier for the parents who work in businesses and don't have the summer to be with their children.

    b. The regular school schedule requires that students attend classes from September to June.

    c. Both year-round school and regular school schedules are found throughout the United States.

    d. With year-round school, students attend classes for nine weeks, and then have three weeks' vacation.

10. The author feels that
   a. each school should decide what schedule to follow.
   b. year-round school is better.
   c. both year-round and regular school schedules have different advantages and disadvantages.
   d. the regular school schedule is better.

11. The main organizing principle of this passage is
   a. chronology.
   b. order of importance.
   c. comparison and contrast.
   d. cause and effect.

A SIBLING RIVALRY

You will need to know the following words as you read the story:

tandem: working together
maneuver: make a series of changes in direction

The man with the bullhorn encouraged the runners as they made their way up the hill. "Two hours, fifteen minutes, forty seconds . . ." His deep, amplified voice boomed toward us.

It was mile 17 of the marathon.

"Hey, great stride!" a bearded spectator yelled to me. He clapped loudly. "You're looking strong. Keep going—go, go, go!"

You betcha I'm looking strong, I thought, as I followed my younger sister, Laura. I just got started. She had been diligently clocking eight-minute miles since the race had begun downtown. Initially in the middle of a pack, which was several thousand people, she had been steadily passing other runners for the past 10 miles or so. We were now on the relatively steep rise to the St. Cecelia Bridge. Once we crossed, we would begin heading back into town, running along the east side of the Rincon River. Laura had asked me to run the most difficult section of the marathon with her. Not having trained for anything more challenging than a brisk walk, and with no experience running in organized events, I figured I might be good for two or three miles.

Despite our running in tandem, we were taking different approaches to the event. Laura was on an aggressive tack, maneuvering quickly through the slowing pack of runners. She began calling out, "On your left, sir," and "Excuse me," as she doggedly yet gracefully attacked the rising slope approaching the bridge. Keeping up with her was no small feat. On one hand, I felt like saying to her, Wait up! On the other hand, I knew that a timely finish would be a personal record for her.

Up ahead, steel drums were playing. A group of percussionists was pounding out rhythms, chanting, and encouraging us with their music and smiles. Crossing the bridge, I recalled the advice in the Marathon Handbook to be sure to spit off of the steely span. During my preview of the route, it had seemed like a juvenile thing to do. But now it seemed like a fine idea, and I spat magnificently over the side of the bridge.

"I read the handbook, too!" trumpeted a triumphant woman behind me, who also let loose over the side of the bridge. We had now initiated a chain reaction of subsequent bridge spitters. It was quite a sight, but I had other things to occupy my attention, namely the back of Laura's jersey.

Easing off the bridge, and heading south on Avila Boulevard, Laura and I found our pace together again. Here we could hang to the left of the group and enjoy some brief conversation. "You keeping up okay?" she asked. Being her older brother, and therefore unable to admit weakness, I nodded convincingly.

"Hey, Lee!" yelled a waving man on the sidewalk. Immediately pleased that my marathon efforts had been recognized by someone I knew, I waved back and reflected on the importance of wearing tie-dyed clothing to a road race of this size. It made it a lot easier to be spotted!

The town marathon is a "people's" marathon in that it tends to be a family affair, with the runners and spectators creating a festival atmosphere. The crowds are demonstrably vocal and supportive all day, which means a lot to the participants. I managed to run six miles before bowing out, and Laura finished the entire race in under four hours.

I now pride myself on telling people that I ran in a marathon. The distinction between having run a marathon and having run in a marathon seems unimportant. If pressed, however, I'll admit that I only ran one-fourth of one.

Inspired by this year's experience, I plan to walk the course—really fast—next year. It's not because I'm jealous of my sister's accomplishment. This is not some silly sibling rivalry in which I must do whatever she does. Rather, Laura got free cookies at the finish line, and the promise of that will lead me to any goal.

QUESTIONS

12. This story is told from the point of view of
 a. Laura.
 b. Lee.
 c. both Laura and Lee.
 d. an unidentified, third-person narrator.

13. Read these sentences from the story.

Laura was on an aggressive tack, maneuvering quickly through the slowing pack of runners. She began calling out, "On your left, sir," and "Excuse me," as she doggedly yet gracefully attacked the rising slope approaching the bridge.

Below are four definitions of **tack.** Which one probably means the same as the word is used in this section of the passage?

 a. a sharp-pointed nail
 b. something that attaches
 c. a sticky or adhesive quality
 d. a zigzag movement

14. What happened immediately AFTER Lee spit over the side of the bridge?
 a. Laura was embarrassed.
 b. A woman spat over the bridge.
 c. Lee apologized for his manners.
 d. Lee saw someone that he knew.

15. Why did the author write this story?
 a. to explain how marathons are won
 b. to tell about the history of marathons
 c. to tell a story about a marathon experience
 d. to show how difficult running in a marathon can be

16. Why was Lee glad he wore a tie-dyed shirt?

a. It helped people locate him easily.

b. The shirt brought him good luck.

c. It added to the festival atmosphere.

d. The shirt was a favorite of Laura's.

17. What part of the marathon does Laura ask Lee to run?

a. the last six miles

b. the downhill section

c. the most difficult section

d. the last two to three miles

18. At next year's marathon, Lee plans to

a. run half of the course.

b. beat his sister Laura.

c. walk the race really fast.

d. improve his time.

19. Which of the following words best describes Laura as she is presented in this passage?

a. competitive

b. foolish

c. comical

d. carefree

20. The author wants the reader to think that Lee

a. is too aggressive.

b. has little self-confidence.

c. has a future as a runner.

d. is a good-natured brother.

21. Lee tells Laura that he's keeping up okay because

a. he doesn't want her to think he can't keep up with her.

b. he is always lying to her.

c. he really *is* doing okay.

d. he wants to motivate her.

22. The tone of this passage is best described as

a. tense and anxious.

b. light and friendly.

c. matter-of-fact.

d. uninterested and bored.

JOURNEY TO A NEW LIFE

For hundreds of years, people have come to the United States from other countries seeking a better life. One of the first sights to greet many immigrants is the Statue of Liberty. This is the story of Tatiana and her journey to the United States.

In 1909, when Tatiana was just 11 years old, her parents and older brother traveled to the United States. Because the family could not afford to buy her a ticket, she had to remain in Russia. She had lived with her uncle and cousins for almost a year in a small and crowded house before the special letter arrived from her father. "Dear Tatiana," he wrote. "At last we have earned enough money to pay for your ticket. After you join us in New York, we will travel by train to a place called South Dakota where we have bought a farm."

A week later, Tatiana's uncle took her into the city of St. Petersburg, and using the money her father had sent, bought her a ticket for the *Louisa Jane*, a steamship that was leaving for America. Tatiana clutched her bag nervously and walked up the ramp onto the steamship that would be her home until she reached America. She listened to the ship's whistle give a piercing blast and then leaned over the railing to wave good-bye to her uncle.

Although she was lonely and missed her family, Tatiana quickly made friends with the other children aboard the *Louisa Jane*. Together, they invented games that could be played on the ship, and they ran around the decks. One afternoon, tired of being pestered with questions, the ship's engineer gave them a tour of the engines.

The next day, as Tatiana was walking along the deck, she heard some of the passengers talking about the Statue of Liberty. This conversation confused her because she knew that liberty was an idea; it was intangible. No one could see or touch it, so how could you make a statue of liberty? When she asked her friend's father, Mr. Dimitrivitch, he explained that the statue looked like a woman, but it represented freedom. This explanation just made Tatiana more curious to see the statue for herself.

One morning, Tatiana woke up to the sound of wild shouting. Convinced that the ship must be sinking, she grabbed her lifejacket and ran upstairs. All of the passengers were crowded onto the deck, but the ship wasn't sinking. The shouts were really cries of excitement because the *Louisa Jane* had finally reached the United States. When Tatiana realized that she would soon see her family again, she joined in with shouts of her own.

As the *Louisa Jane* came closer to shore, the tall figure of a woman holding a torch became visible on the horizon. The cries died away and the passengers stared in awed silence at the Statue of Liberty. Tatiana gazed at the woman's solemn face as the ship steamed past. Mr. Dimitrivitch had told her that the statue represented freedom, and she finally understood what he meant. At that moment, Tatiana knew that she was free to start her new life.

QUESTIONS

23. For Tatiana, the Statue of Liberty was a symbol of
  a. a new beginning.
  b. interesting ideas.
  c. the excitement of traveling.
  d. the ability to earn money.

24. Which words in the story tell the reader that these events took place long ago?
  a. "...stared in awed silence at the Statue of Liberty"
  b. "...a steamship that was leaving for the United States"
  c. "...she was lonely and missed her family..."
  d. "...Tatiana's uncle took her into the city..."

25. The engineer showed the children the ship's engines because
  a. he was tired of answering their many questions.
  b. the parents asked him to amuse their children.
  c. Tatiana had asked him to do so.
  d. the tour was included in the price of the tickets.

26. The best way to learn more about the kind of ship described in this story would be to
  a. ask someone who builds sailboats.
  b. read a book about the immigrants in New York.
  c. visit a port where large ships dock.
  d. look in an encyclopedia under Steamships.

27. Which emotion did the passengers on the ship feel when they saw the statue?

    a. excitement

    b. awe

    c. loneliness

    d. regret

28. Why did the author write this story?

    a. to describe a particular statue

    b. to express the author's opinion

    c. to persuade the reader to take an action

    d. to describe one person's experience

EXCERPT FROM "FIRST," A SHORT STORY

First, you ought to know that I'm "only" fourteen. My mother points this out often. I can make my own decisions when I'm old enough to vote, she says. Second, I should tell you that she's right—I'm not always responsible. I sometimes take the prize for grade-A dork. Take last weekend, for instance. I was staying at Dad's, and I decided it was time I learned to drive. It was Sunday morning, 7 A.M., and I hadn't slept well. I'd been up thinking about an argument, which I'll tell you about in a minute. Well, nobody was up yet in the neighborhood, so I thought it couldn't hurt to back the car out of the garage and drive around the block. But Dad has a clutch car. The R on the shift handle was up on the left side, right next to first gear. I guess you can guess the rest.

Dad's always been understanding. He didn't say, "Okay, little Miss Know-It-All, you can just spend the rest of the year paying this off," which is what Mom would have said. Instead, Dad worried about what might have happened to me. To me. And that made me feel more guilty than anything. I think he'd be a better number-one caregiver, but I can't say things like that to Mom. To her, I have to say, "But Mom, Dad's place is closer to school. I could ride my bike."

To which she replies, "Amy Lynn, you don't own a bike. Remember? You left it in the yard, and it was stolen. And you haven't got the patience to earn the money to replace it."

QUESTIONS

29. How does the narrator show how she feels about her dad and mom?

    a. through specific detail

    b. by asking questions that make a point but don't invite a direct answer

    c. through similes and metaphors

    d. by contrasting her parents' typical reactions

30. The first-person point of view in this story

    a. hides the narrator's feelings.

    b. shows the thoughts and personality of the narrator.

    c. makes the narrator seem cold and distant.

    d. lets you hear the thoughts of all the characters.

31. The narrator feels guilty because she
  a. made her dad worry.
  b. ruined the car.
  c. broke the law.
  d. didn't tell her mom about the car incident.

32. The narrator says she "sometimes take[s] the prize for a grade-A dork." This word choice means to show
  a. that she doesn't know proper English.
  b. that she can't judge her own actions.
  c. her age and culture.
  d. that she thinks she's better than other "dorks."

33. The quotation marks around "only" suggest that the narrator
  a. is almost fifteen.
  b. thinks fourteen is old enough for some things.
  c. wishes she were older.
  d. thinks fourteen is a lousy age.

34. The narrator's tone is
  a. emotional and familiar.
  b. stuck up and superior.
  c. angry and sad.
  d. pleasant and charming.

35. The main conflict between the narrator and her mother is about whether she
  a. can make her own decisions.
  b. should live with her mom or her dad.
  c. should be allowed to drive.
  d. should pay for things she loses or breaks.

36. The narrator's mom thinks the narrator is
  a. too attached to her dad.
  b. too emotional.
  c. too shy.
  d. irresponsible.

37. The narrator feels that her mom
  a. is too busy to care for her.
  b. should never have divorced her dad.
  c. makes too many rules.
  d. cares more about things than about people.

38. What most likely happened with the car?
  a. The narrator put the car in first gear instead of reverse. She ran into the garage wall.
  b. The narrator backed out of the driveway and into a neighbor's car.
  c. The narrator left the car in gear when she was done. When her dad started the car, he ran into the garage wall.
  d. The narrator broke the clutch while trying to shift gears.

OFFICE

My "office" measures a whopping 5 feet by 7 feet. A large desk is squeezed into one corner, leaving just enough room for a rickety chair between the desk and the wall. Yellow paint is peeling off the walls in dirty chunks. The ceiling is barely six feet tall; it's like a hat that I wear all day long. The window, a single two-foot by two-foot pane, looks out onto a solid brick wall just two feet away.

QUESTIONS

39. The main idea of this paragraph is that
    a. the office is small but comfortable.
    b. the office is in need of repair.
    c. the office is old and claustrophobic.
    d. the narrator deserves a better office.

40. The sentence "it's like a hat that I wear all day long" is an example of which literary device?
    a. simile
    b. metaphor
    c. alliteration
    d. personification

ANSWERS

If you missed any of the questions, you can find help with that kind of question in the lesson(s) shown to the right of the answer.

Question	Answer	Lesson(s)	Question	Answer	Lesson(s)
1	a	2, 16	21	a	1, 17
2	b	1, 4	22	b	14
3	b	1, 4	23	a	19
4	c	1, 4	24	b	1, 12
5	d	2	25	a	17
6	b	1, 12	26	d	1, 4
7	a	1, 4	27	b	12, 19
8	b	3	28	d	11, 16
9	a	4	29	d	8, 19
10	c	2	30	b	11
11	c	8	31	a	19
12	b	11	32	c	12
13	d	3	33	b	12, 13
14	b	1, 6	34	a	14
15	c	11, 16	35	a	17, 19
16	a	1, 4	36	d	19
17	c	1, 4	37	d	19
18	c	1, 4	38	a	17
19	a	12	39	c	16
20	d	12, 16	40	a	13, 19

S·E·C·T·I·O·N 1

BUILDING A STRONG FOUNDATION

 eaders are a lot like detectives. To be a good detective, you need a few basic skills. Likewise, you must master a few basic skills for reading success. These skills are your foundation, your building blocks for reading success.

By the end of Section 1, you should know four basic reading comprehension skills:

- how to be an active reader
- how to find the main idea of a passage
- how to figure out what words mean without a dictionary
- how to tell the difference between fact and opinion

L·E·S·S·O·N

BECOMING AN ACTIVE READER

1

LESSON SUMMARY

The most important thing you can do to improve your reading skills is to become an **active reader.** This lesson shows you how to read carefully and actively so that you can better understand and remember what you read.

f you want to earn a high score on a video game, you need to concentrate all of your attention on the game. You need to watch the whole screen carefully and look out for what's coming up ahead. You need to look for certain clues and be able to predict what will happen. In other words, you need to be fully engaged with the game to win.

It sounds a lot like the formula for reading success.

To understand and remember what you read, you need to be involved with what you are reading. In other words, you need to be an active reader. People often think of reading as a passive activity. After all, you're just sitting there, looking at words on a page. But when you read, you should actually be *interacting with* the text.

Five specific strategies will help you become an active reader:

1. skimming ahead and jumping back
2. highlighting or underlining key words and ideas
3. looking up unfamiliar vocabulary words
4. recording your questions and comments
5. looking for clues throughout the text

SKIM AHEAD AND JUMP BACK

Skimming ahead enables you to see what's coming up. Before you begin reading, scan the text to see what's ahead. Is the reading broken up into sections? What are the main topics of those sections? In what order are they covered? What key words or ideas are boldfaced, bulleted, boxed, or otherwise highlighted?

> Skimming through a text before you read helps you prepare for your reading task. It's a lot like checking out the course before a cross-country race. If you know what's ahead, you know how to pace yourself. This head start will give you an idea of what's important in the passage you're about to read.

When you finish reading, **jump back.** Review the summaries, headings, and highlighted information. (This includes both what you and the author highlighted.) Jumping back helps you remember the information you just read. You can see how each idea fits into the whole and how ideas and information are connected.

PRACTICE 1

Just to test yourself, skim ahead through Lesson 2. Look at the summaries, headings, and other reading aids. Then answer the questions below.
Questions

1. What is the main thing you will learn in Lesson 2?

   _____

   _____

2. What are the main topics of Lesson 2? _____

   _____

   _____

3. What key words or phrases are defined in Lesson 2?

   _____

   _____

FINDING KEY WORDS AND IDEAS

In any text, some facts and ideas are more important than others. To be an active reader, you need to identify key ideas. By highlighting or underlining the key words and ideas, you'll make important information stand out. You'll also make it easier to find that information when you want to write a summary or to study for an exam.

Of course, to highlight key words and ideas, you must be able to determine which facts and ideas are most important. Ask yourself: What's the most important information to understand and remember?

Here are two guidelines for highlighting or underlining a text (you'll learn a lot more about this in the next lesson when you learn how to determine the main idea):

1. **Be selective.** If you highlight four sentences in a five-sentence paragraph, you haven't helped yourself at all. The key is to identify what's most important in that passage. Ask yourself two questions:
   a. What is the author trying to say and what is the main idea of his or her passage?
   b. What information is emphasized or seems to stand out as important?

   You can also highlight information that you find particularly interesting.

2. **Watch for clues** that indicate an idea is important. Words and phrases like *most important, the key is,* and *significantly* signal that key information will follow. Watch for visual clues, too. Key

words and ideas are often boldfaced, under-lined, or italicized. They may be boxed in or repeated in a sidebar.

PRACTICE 2

Lesson 2 will show you how to identify topic sentences and main ideas. Meanwhile, you can do your best and practice looking for verbal and visual clues.

Questions

Read the paragraph below, *twice*, and highlight the most important information.

Wind Chill Factor

People have known for a long time that they feel colder when the wind is blowing. The reason for this is simple. The faster the wind blows, the faster your body will lose heat. To educate the public, scientists in Antarctica performed experiments and developed a table to give people a better idea of how cold they would feel outside when the wind was blowing. This is important because prolonged exposure to cold temperatures can be dangerous.

LOOK UP UNFAMILIAR WORDS

Looking up unfamiliar words is another very important active reading strategy. You need to know what the words mean to understand what someone is saying. After all, a key word or phrase can change the meaning of a whole passage.

Whenever possible, have a dictionary with you when you read. Circle and look up any unfamiliar words right away. (Circling them makes them easier to find if you lose your place.) Write the meaning in the margin. That way, you won't have to look up the meaning again if you forget it; it will always be there to refer to. (Of course, if you don't own the book, don't write in it! Instead, write down the vocabulary word and its definition in a notebook.)

If you don't have a dictionary with you, try to figure out what the word means. What clues does the author provide in that sentence and surrounding sentences? Mark the page number or write down the word somewhere so you can look it up later. See how closely you were able to guess its meaning. (You'll learn more about this in Lesson 3.)

PRACTICE 3

Questions

Read the paragraph below carefully. Circle any unfamiliar words, and then look them up in the dictionary. Write their meanings below or in the margins. Then reread the paragraph to fully understand its meaning.

We'd just moved to South Mountain, and I didn't know anyone in the neighborhood. On my first day at South Mountain High, I was petrified. I'm shy to begin with, you know, so you can imagine how I felt walking into that strange school. I wore my favorite outfit to bolster my confidence, but it didn't help much. It seemed like everyone was staring at me, but it was probably just my imagination running rampant, as usual. In fact, I thought I was imagining things when I walked into my new homeroom. I couldn't believe my eyes! There, sitting in the front row, was Maggie Rivers, my best friend from Oakwood Elementary School.

RECORD YOUR QUESTIONS AND COMMENTS

As you read, you're bound to have questions and comments. You're also likely to have reactions to the reading. You might wonder why the author used a certain example, or you might think a particular description is beautiful. Write your questions and comments in the margin (or on a separate piece of paper if the book is not yours) using the code that follows.

Place a **?** in the margin if you have a question about the text or if there is something that you don't understand.

Place a **✓** in the margin if you agree with what the author wrote.

Place an **X** in the margin if you disagree with what the author wrote.

Place a **+** if you see connections between the text and other texts you have read, or if you understand the experience being described.

Place an **!** in the margin if you are surprised by the text or the writer's style.

Place a **☺** in the margin if there is something you read that you like about the text or the style.

Place a **☹** in the margin if there is something you read that you don't like about the text or the style.

This kind of note taking keeps you actively involved with your reading. It makes you think more carefully about what you read—and that means you will better understand and remember the material.

Here's an example of how you might respond to the Wind Chill Factor passage:

Wind Chill Factor

+ People have known for a long time that they feel colder when the wind is blowing. The reason
✓ for this is simple. The faster the wind blows, the faster your body will lose heat. To educate the public, scientists in Antarctica performed experiments and developed a table to give people a **☹** better idea of how cold they would feel outside when the wind was blowing. This is important because prolonged exposure to cold temperatures can be dangerous. **?**

As you used this shorthand, you would know that:

The **+** next to the first line means that you remember the cold temperatures on your school ski trip last February.

The **✓** next to the second line means that you know that cold winds make your body lose heat.

The **☹** next to the third line means that you wish the author had included the table to make the point more clear.

The **?** next to the fifth line means that you don't know how long is "prolonged."

PRACTICE 4
Questions

Reread the passage from Practice 3, reprinted here. Record your own questions and comments.

> We'd just moved to South Mountain, and I didn't know anyone in the neighborhood. On my first day at South Mountain High, I was petrified. I'm shy to begin with, you know, so you can imagine how I felt walking into that strange school. I wore my favorite outfit to bolster my confidence, but it didn't help much. It seemed like everyone was staring at me, but it was probably just my imagination running rampant, as usual. In fact, I thought I was imagining things when I walked into my new homeroom. I couldn't believe my eyes! There, sitting in the front row, was Maggie Rivers, my best friend from Oakwood Elementary School.

LOOKING FOR CLUES

We've already mentioned the word "clues" a couple of times in this lesson. That's because good readers are a lot like detectives. They don't read just to get through a passage; they pay careful attention to words and details, much like Sherlock Holmes would do if he were solving a mystery. Detectives look for clues that will help them better understand the writer's ideas. These clues come in many forms such as:

- specific word choice and details
- repeated words or phrases
- the structure of sentences or paragraphs

The key to finding these clues is to *look carefully*. Be observant. As you read, keep your eyes open. Look not just at what the writer is saying, but also in *how* he or she says it. *Notice* the words he or she uses. *Look* at how the ideas are organized.

Being observant is essential for reading success. People draw conclusions (make *inferences*) about what they read, and sometimes those conclusions are wrong. Usually this means that they just didn't read carefully enough. They didn't notice the clues the writer left for them, and they based their conclusions on their *own* ideas. But conclusions should be based on the ideas that are there in the text.

The rest of this book will give you specific strategies for recognizing these clues.

SUMMARY

Active reading is the key to reading success. Active readers use the following strategies:

1. skimming ahead and jumping back
2. highlighting or underlining key words and ideas
3. looking up unfamiliar vocabulary words
4. recording their questions and comments
5. looking for clues not just in what the writer says, but in *how* he or she says it

Skill Building until Next Time

Here are some ways to practice the skills you've learned in this lesson. Practice them today and the rest of the week:

1. Write a quick note or e-mail to a friend and explain what "active reading" means. Describe the strategies that active readers use to better understand and remember what they read.

2. Develop a detective's eye. Notice the things around you. Look at the details on people's faces and clothing. Notice the names of the stores you pass on your way to school. Pay close attention to the things around you. You may be surprised at the interesting things you see that you hadn't noticed before. To test yourself, write down the names of all the stores on the block where you walk every day, or jot down the colors of all the houses on the street where you live.

3. Try your active reading strategies when you read your favorite magazine.

ANSWERS

PRACTICE 1

1. The main thing you will learn in Lesson 2 is how to identify the main idea of a passage.
2. The main topics of Lesson 2 are the definition of **main idea, topic sentence,** and **main ideas in paragraphs and essays.**
3. The key words and phrases defined in Lesson 2 are **main idea, subject, assertion,** and **topic sentence.**

PRACTICE 2

You should have highlighted or underlined as follows:

Wind Chill Factor

People have known for a long time that they feel colder when the wind is blowing. The reason for this is simple. <u>The faster the wind blows, the faster your body will lose heat</u>. To educate the public, scientists in Antarctica performed experiments and developed a table to give people a better idea of how cold they would feel outside when the wind was blowing. This is important because <u>prolonged exposure to cold temperatures can be dangerous</u>.

The first underlined sentence is important because it explains why the wind chill factor exists. Notice that the second underlined sentence begins with the signal phrase "This is important." This tells us that this fact is significant and should be highlighted.

PRACTICE 3

You probably circled the words *petrified, bolster,* and *rampant.*

- *To petrify* means to change or cause to change into a stony mass; to paralyze or stun with fear. The author of this paragraph is using the second meaning of the word.
- *To bolster* means to support or prop up; to strengthen.
- *Rampant* means unrestrained; going beyond normal limits; unchecked or excessive.

Now that you know the definitions, reread the paragraph. Does it take on a new meaning for you?

PRACTICE 4

Answers will vary. Here's one possibility:

+ We'd just moved to South Mountain, and I didn't know anyone in the neighborhood. On my first day at South Mountain High, I was petrified. I'm shy to begin with, you know, so you can imagine how I felt walking into that strange school. I wore my favorite outfit to bolster my confidence, but it didn't help much. It seemed like everyone was staring at me, but it was ✓
! probably just my imagination running rampant, as usual. In fact, I thought I was imagining things when I walked into my new homeroom. I couldn't believe my eyes! There, sitting in the front row, was Maggie Rivers, my best friend from Oakwood Elementary School.

As you use this shorthand, you would know that:

The **+** next to the first sentence means you understand what it means to be petrified. You may have been through a similar experience.

The **✓** next to the third sentence means that you know how important it is to boost self-confidence.

The **!** next to the fifth sentence means that you are surprised that the narrator's reaction had run rampant.

L·E·S·S·O·N

FINDING THE MAIN IDEA

2

LESSON SUMMARY

Finding and understanding the main idea of a text is an essential reading skill. When you look past the facts and information and get to the heart of what the writer is trying to say, that's the main idea. This lesson will show you how to find the main idea of a passage. Then you'll learn how to distinguish the main idea from its supporting statements.

magine that you're at a friend's home for the evening. "Here," he says, "Let's watch this movie."

"Sure," you reply. "What's it about?" You'd like to know a little about what you'll be watching, but your question may not get you the answer you're looking for. That's because you've only asked about the *subject* of the film. The subject—what the movie is *about*—is only half the story. Think, for example, about all the alien invaders films that have been made. While these films may share the same general subject, what they have to say *about* the aliens (and about our response to invasion) may be very different. Each film has different ideas it wants to convey *about* the subject.

Similarly, writers write because they have something they want to write *about*, and they have something they want to say *about* that subject. When you look beyond the facts and information to what the writer really wants to say *about* his or her subject, you're looking for the **main idea**.

JUST WHAT IS A MAIN IDEA, ANYWAY?

One of the most common questions on reading comprehension exams is, "What is the main idea of this passage?" How would you answer this question for the paragraph below?

Wilma Rudolph, the crippled child who became an Olympic running champion, is an inspiration for us all. Born prematurely in 1940, Wilma spent her childhood battling illness, including measles, scarlet fever, chicken pox, pneumonia, and polio, a crippling disease which at that time had no cure. At the age of four, she was told she would never walk again. But Wilma and her family refused to give up. After years of special treatment and physical therapy, 12-year-old Wilma was able to walk normally again. But walking wasn't enough for Wilma, who was determined to be an athlete. Before long, her talent earned her a spot in the 1956 Olympics, where she earned a bronze medal. In the 1960 Olympics, the height of her career, she won three gold medals.

What is the main idea of this paragraph? You might be tempted to answer, "Wilma Rudolph" or "Wilma Rudolph's life." Yes, Wilma Rudolph's life is the **subject** of the passage—*who or what the passage is about.* But that's not the main idea. The **main idea** is what the writer wants to say *about* this subject. What is the main thing the writer says *about* Wilma's life?

Before we answer that question, let's review the definition of *main idea:*

Main idea: The overall fact, feeling, or thought a writer wants to convey about his or her subject.

We call this the main idea because it is the idea that the passage *adds up to;* it's what holds all of the ideas in the passage together. Now, reread the paragraph about Wilma Rudolph carefully. Which idea holds the paragraph together?

a. Wilma Rudolph was very sick as a child.
b. Wilma Rudolph was an Olympic champion.
c. Wilma Rudolph is someone to admire.

The best answer is **c**: Wilma Rudolph is someone to admire. This is the idea the paragraph adds up to; it's what holds all of the information in the paragraph together.

This example also shows us two important characteristics of a main idea:

1. It is **general** enough to encompass all of the ideas in the passage.
2. It is an **assertion.** An assertion is a statement made by the writer.

MAIN IDEAS ARE GENERAL

The main idea of a passage must be general enough to encompass all of the ideas in the passage. That is, it should be broad enough for all of the other sentences in that passage to fit underneath it, like people under an umbrella. Notice that the first two options, "Wilma Rudolph was very sick as a child" and "Wilma Rudolph was an Olympic champion" are too specific to be the main idea. They aren't broad enough to cover all of the ideas in the passage, because the passage talks about *both* her illnesses and her Olympic achievements. Only the third answer is general enough to be the main idea of the paragraph.

EXERCISE 1
Questions

In the group of sentences below, circle the sentence that is general enough to be a main idea.

    a. The Gold Rush began in 1849.

    b. Many people moved to California after gold was discovered.

    c. The history and population of California were shaped by the Gold Rush.

    d. The life of a gold miner was not an easy one.

MAIN IDEAS ARE ASSERTIONS

A main idea is also some kind of **assertion** about the subject. An assertion is a claim that something is true. An assertion, therefore, needs to be supported with specific details or evidence. Assertions can be facts (such as "Wind chills can be dangerous.") or opinions (such as "School uniforms for public school students are a bad idea."). In either case, an assertion should be supported by specific ideas, facts, and details. In other words, the main idea makes a general assertion that *tells* readers that something is true. The supporting sentences, on the other hand, *show* readers that it's true by providing specific facts and details.

For example, in the Wilma Rudolph paragraph, the writer makes a general assertion: "Wilma Rudolph, the crippled child who became an Olympic running champion, is an inspiration for us all." The rest of the sentences offer specific facts and details that *prove* that Wilma Rudolph is an inspirational person.

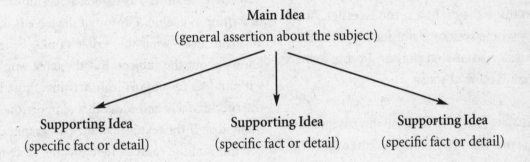

Main Idea
(general assertion about the subject)

Supporting Idea
(specific fact or detail)

Supporting Idea
(specific fact or detail)

Supporting Idea
(specific fact or detail)

EXERCISE 2
Questions

Which of the following sentences are assertions that require specific evidence or support?

    a. Blue is a color.

    b. Blue is a calming color.

    c. Ray Bradbury is a fabulous science fiction writer.

    d. Ray Bradbury published *The Illustrated Man* in 1951.

    e. Ray Bradbury's best book is *The Illustrated Man.*

TOPIC SENTENCES

Writers often state their main ideas in one or two sentences so that readers can be very clear about the main point of the passage. A sentence that expresses the main idea of a paragraph is called a **topic sentence**. Notice, for example, how the first sentence in the Wilma Rudolph paragraph states the main idea:

Wilma Rudolph, the crippled child who became an Olympic running champion, *is an inspiration for us all.*

This sentence is therefore the topic sentence for the paragraph.

Topic sentences are often found at the beginning of paragraphs. But not all paragraphs begin with a clear topic sentence. Sometimes writers begin with specific supporting ideas and lead up to the main idea. In this case, the topic sentence is often found at the end of the paragraph. Here's an example:

School is tough enough without having to worry about looking cool every single day. The less I have to decide first thing in the morning, the better. I can't tell you how many mornings I look into my closet and just stare, unable to decide what to wear. I also wouldn't mind not having to see guys wearing oversized jeans and shirts so huge they'd fit a sumo wrestler. And I certainly would welcome not seeing kids showing off designer-labeled clothes. To me, a dress code makes a lot of sense.

Notice how the last sentence in this paragraph is the only one that is general enough to cover the entire paragraph. Each sentence in the paragraph provides specific support for the final assertion: A dress code is a good idea.

Sometimes the topic sentence is not found at the beginning or end of a paragraph but rather somewhere in the middle. Other times there isn't a clear topic sentence at all. But that doesn't mean there isn't a main idea. It's there, but the author has chosen not to express it in a clear topic sentence. In that case, you'll have to look carefully at the paragraph for clues about the main idea. You'll learn more about this in Section 4.

MAIN IDEAS IN PARAGRAPHS AND ESSAYS

We often talk about a text as having *one* main idea. But if the text has more than one paragraph, shouldn't it have as many main ideas as it has paragraphs? Yes and no. Each *paragraph* should have its own main idea. In fact, that's the definition of a paragraph: a group of sentences about the same idea. At the same time, however, each paragraph does something more: It works to support the main idea of the *entire passage*. Thus, there is an **overall main idea** (often called a **theme** or **thesis**) for the text. The main idea of *each paragraph* should work to support the overall main idea of the entire text.

Here's another way to look at it. Think of a piece of writing as a table. The top of the table is the overall main idea—what the writer thinks, believes, or knows about the subject. But the table won't stand without legs to support it. In writing, those legs are the specific facts and ideas that support the overall main idea. If the text is just one paragraph, then we can think of the topic sentence as the table top and the supporting sentences as the table legs. If the text is several paragraphs (or pages) long, then we have a series of tables on top of tables. Each leg is actually its own paragraph. It has its own main idea and therefore needs supporting sentences of its own. Indeed, depending upon the length of the text, there may be tables on top of tables on top of tables—layers of main ideas and their support. But there will still be that one table on the very top. This is the overall main idea that encompasses all of the ideas in the essay.

DISTINGUISHING MAIN IDEAS FROM SUPPORTING IDEAS

If you're not sure whether something is a main idea or a supporting idea, ask yourself the following question: Is the sentence making a *general statement*, or is it providing *specific information*? In the school uniform paragraph, for example, all of the sentences except the last, make specific statements. They are not general enough to serve as an umbrella or net for the whole paragraph.

> Writers often provide clues that can help you distinguish between main ideas and their support. Here are some of the most common words and phrases used to introduce specific examples:
>
> | | | |
> |---|---|---|
> | for example | in addition | some |
> | for instance | in particular | specifically |
> | furthermore | others | |

These signal words tell you that a supporting fact or idea will follow. If you're having trouble finding the main idea of a paragraph, try eliminating sentences that begin with these phrases.

EXERCISE 3

Read the passage below carefully using the skills taught in this lesson. After you read, answer the questions that follow. Keep in mind that you'll be asked to identify not only the overall main idea, but also the main idea of individual paragraphs.

At the age of six, Goran Kropp climbed his first mountain. Twenty-three years later, he tackled one of the highest mountains in the world, Mount Everest. His journey to the top shows just how independent, persistent, and determined this remarkable man is.

While most people arrive at the foothills of Mount Everest by some sort of modern vehicle, Kropp bicycled 7,000 miles from his home in Sweden. Traveling by bike was not easy. Bumpy, rough roads caused mechanical problems for Kropp, and he stopped many times to repair his bike. In addition, he was chased by dogs, stung by hornets, and drenched by rain several times before he arrived at the base of the mountain.

Kropp chose to climb Mount Everest the same way he traveled to the mountain: without the help of others and without modern conveniences. Unlike others, Kropp climbed the mountain without a guide or helper. He did not bring bottled oxygen to help him breathe at high altitudes, and he carried all of his gear himself in a pack that weighed about 140 pounds.

It took Kropp two tries to reach the summit. The first time, he had to turn back only 350 feet from the top because the weather was too dangerous. Just a few days earlier, at that same level, eight climbers had died when a sudden snowstorm had hit the mountain. Kropp waited out the storm, rested, and tried again a few days later. This time, he was successful. When he had finished descending the mountain, he got back on his bike and rode the 7,000 miles back to Sweden.

Questions

Read and answer the following questions.

1. What is the *subject* of this passage? _____

   _____

2. What is the *main idea* of paragraph 2? _____

   _____

   _____

2014 8408

3. What is the *main idea* of paragraph 3? _____

_____

_____

4. What is the *overall main idea* of the passage?

_____

_____

SUMMARY

The **main idea** of a passage is the overall fact, feeling, or idea the author wants to convey *about* the subject. Main ideas are general enough to encompass all of the ideas in the passage. They also make an assertion about the subject that the rest of the passage develops and supports. Main ideas are often stated in *topic sentences*. In longer texts, each paragraph has a main idea (though it may not be explicitly stated), and each main idea works to support the overall main idea of the passage.

Skill Building until Next Time

1. As you read today and throughout the week, notice how texts are divided into paragraphs. Choose one paragraph from your social studies textbook and identify the topic sentence. What idea holds all of the sentences in that paragraph together?

2. Create topic sentences about things that you come across in your day. Make general assertions about people, places, and things. For example, you might say, "Mrs. Elmore is a great teacher." Then, support your assertion. What does she do that makes her a great teacher? Provide several specific examples.

ANSWERS

EXERCISE 1

The only sentence general enough to be the main idea is (c); (a), (b), and (d) are all details about the Gold Rush.

EXERCISE 2

Sentences (b), (c) and (e) are assertions that require support. Sentences (a) and (d), on the other hand, are simple statements of fact that do not require support.

EXERCISE 3

1. The subject is Kropp's journey to the top of Mount Everest.

2. The main idea of paragraph 2 is stated in the second sentence: "Traveling by bike was not easy."

3. The main idea of paragraph 3 is stated in the first sentence: "Kropp chose to climb Mount Everest the same way he traveled to the mountain: without the help of others and without modern conveniences."

4. The overall main idea is stated in the topic sentence at the end of the first paragraph: "His journey to the top shows just how independent, persistent, and determined this remarkable man is."

L·E·S·S·O·N 3

DEFINING VOCABULARY IN CONTEXT

LESSON SUMMARY

Active readers look up unfamiliar words. But what if you don't have a dictionary? In a testing situation, for example, you almost certainly won't be able to look up words you don't know. But you can use context to help you determine meaning. This lesson will show you how.

Often in your reading you will come across words or phrases that are unfamiliar to you. You might be lucky enough to have a dictionary handy to look up that word or phrase. But what if you don't? How can you understand what you're reading if you don't know what all the words mean? Fortunately, you can often use **context** to determine meaning. That is, by looking carefully at the sentences and ideas surrounding an unfamiliar word, you can often figure out exactly what that word means.

HOW TO DETERMINE MEANING FROM CONTEXT

To demonstrate how you can use context to determine what a word means, let's begin with an example. Read the paragraph below carefully and actively.

Andy is the most unreasonable, pigheaded, subhuman life-form in the entire galaxy, and he makes me so angry I could scream! Of course, I love him like a brother. I sort of have to, because he *is* my brother. More than that, he's my twin! That's right. Andy and Amy (that's me) have the same curly hair and dark eyes. Yet though we look alike, we have very different dispositions. You could say that we're opposites. While I'm often quiet and pensive, Andy is loud and doesn't seem to stop to think about anything. Oh, and did I mention that he's the most stubborn person on the planet?

As you read this passage, you probably came across at least two unfamiliar words: *dispositions* and *pensive*. While a dictionary would be helpful, you don't need to look up these words. The paragraph provides enough clues to help you figure out what these words mean.

Let's begin with *dispositions*. In what context is this word used? Let's take another look at the sentence in which it's used and the two sentences that follow:

Yet though we look alike, we have very different *dispositions*. You could say that we're opposites. While I'm often quiet and *pensive*, Andy is loud and doesn't seem to stop to think about anything.

The context here offers several important clues. First, the sentence in which *dispositions* is used tells us something about what dispositions *are not*. The sentence sets up a contrast between the way that Amy and Andy look and their dispositions. This means that dispositions are *not* something physical.

Another clue is the general content of the paragraph. We can tell from the paragraph that *dispositions* have something to do with *who* Andy and Amy are, since the paragraph describes their personalities.

Yet another clue is what follows the sentence in which *dispositions* is used. Amy offers two specific examples of their dispositions: She's quiet and pensive; he's loud and doesn't seem to think much. These are specific examples of personality traits.

By now you should have a pretty good idea of what *dispositions* means. A *disposition* is
   a. a person's physical characteristics.
   b. a person's preferences.
   c. a person's natural qualities or tendencies.

The best answer, of course, is (c), a person's natural qualities or tendencies. While a person's disposition often helps determine his or her preferences, this passage doesn't say anything about what Amy and Andy like to do (or not do). Nor are these characteristics physical. Amy is talking about their personalities.

Now, let's look at the second vocabulary word, *pensive*. Again, the context provides us with strong clues. Amy states that she and Andy "are opposites"—that though they look alike, they have opposite dispositions. She is quiet, and he is loud. Thus, we can expect that the next pair of descriptions will be opposites, too. So we simply have to look at her description of Andy and come up with its opposite. If Andy "doesn't seem to stop to think about anything," then we can assume that Amy spends a lot of time thinking. We can therefore conclude that *pensive* means
   a. intelligent, wise.
   b. deep in thought.
   c. considerate of others.

The best answer is (b), deep in thought. If you spend a lot of time thinking, that may make you wise. But remember, we're looking for the *opposite* of Andy's characteristic, so (a) and (c) can't be the correct answer.

<table><tr><td>

Exam Tip: When you're trying to determine meaning from context on an exam, two strategies can help you find the best answer.

1. First, determine whether the vocabulary word is something positive or negative. If the word is something positive, then eliminate the answers that are negative, and vice versa.

2. Replace the vocabulary word with the remaining answers, one at a time. Does the answer make sense when you read the sentence? If not, you can eliminate that answer.

</td></tr></table>

EXERCISE 1
Questions

Use context to determine the meaning of the italicized words in the sentences below. Circle the letter of the answer you think is correct.

1. He was so nervous that his voice was *quavering*.
   a. thundering, booming confidently
   b. trembling, shaking noticeably
   c. quiet, whispering softly
   d. undecided, unsure

2. By the end of eighth period, I was *famished*. I'd skipped breakfast and had eaten only a pear for lunch.
   a. famous
   b. exhausted
   c. starving
   d. impatient

3. The autographed picture of Roger Clemens turned out to be *bogus*. The man who sold it to me had signed it himself!
   a. fake, false
   b. believable
   c. interesting
   d. overpriced

HOW MUCH CONTEXT DO YOU NEED?

In the passage about Amy and Andy, you would probably have been able to understand the main message even if you hadn't figured out what *dispositions* and *pensive* mean. But sometimes your understanding of a passage depends upon your understanding of a particular word or phrase. Can you understand the following sentence, for example, without understanding what *elated* means?

He was *elated* when he saw his report card.

The trouble with adjectives like *elated* is that it can be hard to figure out what they mean without sufficient context. From this sentence, we can't even tell whether *elated* is something positive or negative. Was he happy or sad? Shocked or unmoved? No matter how good a detective you are, there simply aren't enough clues in this sentence to tell you what this word means, or even whether *elated* is something good or bad. You simply need more context.

Here's the sentence again, this time with more context. Now can you figure out what *elated* means?

He was *elated* when he saw his report card, and he smiled all the way home. He couldn't wait to tell his parents that he'd improved his grade in every class.

From the context, you can tell that *elated* most nearly means

    a. deeply disappointed.

    b. extremely pleased and proud.

    c. indifferent or uncaring.

    d. mildly happy or content.

The best answer is (b), extremely pleased and proud. The context of the sentence makes it clear that *elated* is something good—in fact, something very good. Therefore, answers (a) and (c) are simply not correct, and (d) isn't strong enough. If he can't wait to tell his parents, his emotion is more than just "content." He is clearly very pleased with his improvement.

EXERCISE 2
Questions

Here are a few more passages with italicized vocabulary words. Use the context to determine their meanings. Circle the letter of the answer you think is correct.

1. I accidentally told Nell about her surprise birthday party. What a *blunder!*

    A *blunder* is
    a. a person who can't keep secrets.
    b. an idea.
    c. a mistake.
    d. a get-together.

2. The aquarium was absolutely *teeming* with fish. I don't know how they had room to move.

    Teeming means
    a. full of or present in large numbers.
    b. working together as a group, cooperating.
    c. cloudy or unclear.
    d. gross or disgustingly dirty.

3. Though I do the same thing every day, my volunteer job is anything but *mundane*. The patients really keep me on my toes, and no two days are ever alike!

    Mundane means
    a. exciting and interesting.
    b. dull and boring.
    c. important and meaningful.
    d. unpleasant and distasteful.

EXERCISE 3

We can't emphasize enough the importance of being able to determine word meaning from context. In reading comprehension, everything rests on your ability to understand the ideas in each sentence. If you don't know what a word means, you may completely misunderstand an important sentence—and that means you could misunderstand the whole passage.

So, here's another practice. This one may be more challenging, since these vocabulary words aren't exactly real words!

Take a careful look at one of the most famous poems in the English language, Lewis Carroll's "Jabberwocky." (Lewis Carroll is the author of the classic *Alice in Wonderland*.) Though you won't be able to determine *exactly* what the nonsense words in the poem mean, you should be able to make an educated guess based on their context.

Questions

Here are the first two stanzas of the poem. Read them carefully and then answer the questions that follow. Read the poem twice, at least one of those times out loud. (The lines of the poem are numbered to make the questions easier to follow.)

Jabberwocky

1 'Twas brillig, and the slithy toves
2 Did gyre and gimble in the wabe;
3 All mimsy were the borogoves,
4 And the mome raths outgrabe.

5 "Beware the Jabberwock, my son!
6 The jaws that bite, the claws that catch!
7 Beware the Jubjub bird, and shun
8 The frumious Bandersnatch!"

Questions

Circle the letter of the answer you think is correct.

1. What could *slithy toves* (line 1) be?
a. some sort of food
b. some sort of place
c. some sort of animal
d. some sort of vehicle

2. The *Jabberwock* (line 5) is probably
a. a mean person.
b. a dangerous creature.
c. a harmless bird.
d. a magical animal.

3. What does *shun* (line 7) mean?
a. to avoid, keep away from
b. to capture
c. to make friends with
d. to take care of

4. What does *frumious* (line 8) probably mean?
a. friendly
b. ugly
c. dangerous
d. poor

SUMMARY

Often, you can figure out what unfamiliar words mean from their **context**—the way they are used in a passage. Look carefully at the words and sentences surrounding the unfamiliar word. You'll often find clues that will tell you what the word means. Even if you can't figure out the exact meaning of a word, you can usually tell whether the word means something positive or negative.

Skill Building until Next Time

1. Before you look up any unfamiliar words this week, try to figure out what they mean from their context. For example, if you come across an unfamiliar word while you're surfing the Web, use the context around that word to determine its meaning. After you've made an educated guess based on the context, look each word up in a dictionary. Did you guess correctly?
2. Begin a vocabulary list of the words you look up as you work your way through this book. Many people feel insecure about their reading and writing skills because they have a limited vocabulary. The more words you know, the easier it will be to understand what others are saying and to express what you have to say.

ANSWERS

EXERCISE 1

1. b. If you are nervous, your voice is not likely to be booming and certainly not likely to be confident. You might speak quietly, but "so nervous" suggests that something unusual was happening to his voice.

2. c. The context here clearly suggests that *famished* has something to do with hunger, since the speaker hadn't eaten anything except a pear all day.

3. a. If the seller signed the autograph, then the autograph must be a fake.

EXERCISE 2

1. c. The context tells us that the speaker has made a mistake and spoiled the surprise for Nell.

2. a. The second sentence tells us that the fish tank was extremely crowded; the speaker is surprised that the fish "had room to move." Therefore, the aquarium must have been packed full of fish.

3. b. The speaker tells us her job keeps her "on her toes" and that "no two days are ever alike." This suggests that her job is exciting, despite the fact that she follows a routine. That's why (b) is the best answer. Read the sentence carefully; she is saying that her job is not mundane, so (a) isn't the correct answer.

EXERCISE 3

1. c. Slithy toves could be some sort of animal. The toves "did gyre and gimble," which suggests that they are active and alive. They could also be some sort of bug or plant, but neither of these was listed as an option.

2. b. The Jabberwock is a dangerous creature. You can tell because the speaker says to "beware the Jabberwock" and describes "the jaws that bite, the claws that catch!" This is clearly a beast you want to stay away from!

3. a. Shun means to avoid, to keep away from. This word *is* in the dictionary.

    c. The speaker says to shun the Bandersnatch in the same stanza as he warns against the dangerous Jabberwock and Jubjub bird. The Bandersnatch must also be dangerous, since the listener is told to keep away from it.

DISTINGUISHING BETWEEN FACT AND OPINION

4

LESSON SUMMARY

One of the most important signs of a good reader is the ability to distinguish between *fact* and *opinion*. This lesson will show you how facts are different from opinions and why this difference matters.

s you know from your own experience, sometimes it's really important to know when someone is telling you what they *think*, not what they *know*. For example, let's say your friend wants you to come over, but you'd planned to work on your book report.

"Don't worry," your friend says. "Mr. Billings is really laid back. He won't care if you hand it in late."

You could be in big trouble if you assume that your friend is offering a fact and not just his opinion.

DEFINING FACT AND OPINION

Before we go any further, let's define these two important terms.

Facts are:
- things *known* for certain to have happened.
- things *known* for certain to be true.
- things *known* for certain to exist.

Opinions, on the other hand, are:
- things *believed* to have happened.
- things *believed* to be true.
- things *believed* to exist.

The key difference between fact and opinion lies in the difference between *knowing* and *believing*. Opinions may be *based* on facts, but they are still what people think and believe, not what they know. Opinions are debatable; two different people could have two different opinions about the matter. Facts, however, are not debatable. Two different people would have a hard time debating a fact. They might not agree on how to *interpret* the facts, but they would have to agree on the facts themselves.

Consider this example: "Basketball is more exciting than football." This statement is debatable. You could argue that football is more exciting than basketball, or that they're both equally exciting, or even that they're both dreadfully boring. All of these statements are opinions. But "Basketball is a team sport" is not debatable; it's impossible to disagree with this statement. It's something known to be true. Thus, it's a fact.

ASKING QUESTIONS

A good test for whether something is fact or opinion, then, is to ask yourself two questions:

- Can this statement be debated?
- Is this something known to be true?

If you can answer "Yes" to the first question, it's probably an *opinion*. If you can answer "Yes" to the second question, it's probably a fact. For example, look at the following sentence:

> Our school's policy is that you must have a C average in order to participate in school sports.

Does this topic sentence express a fact or an opinion? Well, is it debatable? Can someone disagree? Probably not. It's a matter of *fact*, something that could be proven by a quick visit to the principal or the athletic department. On the other hand, look at the following claim. (Read it carefully; it's different from the previous example though it looks the same.)

> Our school should have a policy that you must have at least a C average to participate in school sports.

Now, is this something known to be true, or is this something debatable? Clearly, different people can have different opinions on this issue. It's an *opinion*.

LOOKING FOR CLUES

Writers often provide clues when they are expressing a fact or an opinion. Look at the following passage, for example:

I think school days should be extended until 4:00. Many children go home after school to an empty house. These "latchkey children" are often alone for hours until their parents come home from work. In fact, a recent survey in our school district found that more than 50% of fourth graders are home alone for two or more hours a day.

Of these four sentences, three express facts and one expresses an opinion. Can you tell which one is the opinion? It should be pretty easy to spot; after all, the sentence begins with "I think." Of the other three sentences, one offers a clear clue that it is a fact. Like the opinion, it begins with a signal phrase: "In fact."

There are other signal words, too. Opinions are often stated using words like "should," "ought," or "had better," as in the following examples:

- We *should* apologize for being rude.
- He *ought* to return those library books right away.
- I *had better* get to school before I'm late.

Words that show judgment or evaluation, like "good," "bad," "interesting," and "important," usually signal an opinion, too. Here are some examples:

- She is a *great* teacher.
- This was the *most significant* development in the history of science.
- It was a *fascinating* film.

Words and Phrases that Often Signal Opinions

bad	disappointing	good	important	I think	should
best	excellent	great	insignificant	ought	terrible
boring	fascinating	had better	interesting	remarkable	worst

EXERCISE 1
Questions

Determine whether the following sentences express a fact or an opinion. Write **F** for fact or **O** for opinion before each sentence.

_____ **1.** People should spend less time on the Internet and more time with one another.

_____ **2.** The Internet allows people to communicate with friends and strangers all around the world.

_____ **3.** There ought to be better rules for protecting children on the Internet.

_____ **4.** The Internet is an amazing research tool.

_____ **5.** Billie Jean King is a good role model.

_____ **6.** Many children look up to top entertainers and athletes as role models.

_____ **7.** Only a handful of entertainers and athletes are good role models.

_____ **8.** Many professional athletes earn millions of dollars each year.

_____ **9.** Many professional athletes are grossly overpaid.

WHEN FACTS AND OPINIONS ARE MIXED TOGETHER

It's usually easy to determine whether something is fact or opinion when it stands alone as in the sentences above. But what about when you're looking at a whole paragraph or a whole page? Unless you're reading a scientific or technical manual, you'll usually find a *combination* of facts and opinions. In fact, you'll often find fact and opinion together in the same sentence. One of the topic sentences from Lesson 2 is a good example:

> Wilma Rudolph, the crippled child who became an Olympic running champion, is an inspiration for us all.

The first part of the sentence, "Wilma Rudolph, the crippled child who became an Olympic running champion," is a fact. Rudolph *was* crippled by polio as a child, and she did win medals in the 1956 and 1960 Olympics. But the second part of the sentence—that she "is an inspiration for us all"—is an opinion. It's probably not an opinion that many people would disagree with, but someone *could* argue that Rudolph is not an inspiration. Thus, it's an opinion. Here's another example:

> Winston was an absolute genius, but he died without any recognition or reward for his accomplishments.

Here, the first part of the sentence expresses an opinion, while the second part expresses a fact.

FACT AND OPINION WORKING TOGETHER

People have opinions about everything and anything. But some opinions are more reasonable than others. A *reasonable* opinion is one that is supported by relevant facts. That's what most writing is all about. Writers make claims about their subjects, and those claims are often opinions. Then they offer facts to support those opinions. The Wilma Rudolph passage is a perfect example. The writer begins by offering her opinion—that Rudolph is an inspiration. Then she lists the facts of Rudolph's life as *evidence* that Rudolph is an amazing woman.

Good writers offer support for their opinions because they know that opinions are debatable. They know readers will want to see *why* writers think what they do. Most of their evidence will come in the form of facts. Of course, this doesn't mean that readers will agree with the writer's opinion. But an opinion supported by facts is much stronger than an opinion that stands alone or that is supported only by other opinions. For example, read the two paragraphs below. In one, the writer supports her opinion with facts. In the other, she does not. Which paragraph is stronger?

> Many people are scared of snakes, but they shouldn't be. Snakes have an unfair reputation as dangerous animals. People think snakes are poisonous, have big fangs, and have slimy skin. They shouldn't feel that way about snakes. Snakes ought to have a better reputation because they make great pets and are some of the most interesting creatures around. The people who are scared of snakes had better learn more about these reptiles. Snakes aren't dangerous at all.

> Many people are scared of snakes, but most snakes aren't as dangerous as people think they are. There are more than 2,500 different species of snakes around the world, and only a small percentage of those species are poisonous. Only a few species have venom strong enough to actually kill a human being. Statistically, snakes bite only 1,000–2,000 people in the United States each year, and only ten of those bites (that's less than 1%!) result in death. If you think about it, lots of other animals are far more dangerous than snakes. In fact, in this country, more people die from dog bites each year than from snakes.

Why is the second paragraph so much better than the first? Because the second paragraph offers you more than just opinions. It offers opinions *supported* by specific facts and examples. The first paragraph, on the other hand, opens with a fact but then offers several more unsupported opinions. The opinions are debatable because they state what the author *thinks* is true, not what the author *knows* to be true.

IDENTIFYING SPECIFIC FACTS AND DETAILS

In your classes and on your tests, you'll often be expected to identify and recall specific facts and details from what you read. For the passage about snakes, for example, you might be asked a question like the following:

How many species of snakes are there worldwide?
  a. between 1,000 and 2,000
  b. less than 100
  c. less than 2,5000
  d. more than 2,500

There are several numbers in this passage, and if you didn't read carefully, you could easily choose the wrong answer. The correct answer is (d), more than 2,500. This fact is clearly stated in the second sentence.

How do you identify specific facts and details quickly and accurately, especially when you're reading a passage that's several paragraphs long? You can't be expected to remember every detail. But you can be expected to know *where and how to find* specific facts and details.

For example, in the question just mentioned, the key word that will help you find the exact information you need is "species." If you scan the second snakes paragraph for numbers, you can quickly identify the correct answer by finding the sentence with both a number and the word "species."

In addition, you can use the structure of the paragraph to help you find your answer. If you read carefully, you probably noticed that the paragraph talked first about species, then venom, and then bites. Thus you can use your understanding of the structure to guide you to the correct answer. (This paragraph follows a pattern that you'll learn more about in the next section: moving from general to specific information.)

To find specific facts and details, you can use two guidelines:

1. Look for *key* words in the question that you can locate in the passage.
2. Think about the *structure* of the passage and where that information is likely to be located.

EXERCISE 2

This exercise, which features a longer passage, will give you a chance to practice all of the skills you learned in this lesson. Read the passage carefully (don't forget your active reading strategies) and then answer the questions that follow.

The Gateway Arch

The skyline of St. Louis, Missouri, is fairly unremarkable, with one huge exception—the Gateway Arch, which stands on the banks of the Mississippi. Part of the Jefferson National Expansion Memorial, the Arch is an amazing structure built to honor St. Louis' role as the gateway to the West.

In 1947 a group of interested citizens known as the Jefferson National Expansion Memorial Association held a nationwide competition to select a design for a new monument that would celebrate the growth of the United States. Other U.S. monuments are spires, statues, or imposing buildings, but the winner of this contest was a plan for a completely different type of structure. The man who submitted the winning design, Eero Saarinen, later became a famous architect. In designing the Arch, Saarinen wanted to "create a monument which would have lasting significance and would be a landmark of our time."

The Gateway Arch is a masterpiece of engineering, a monument even taller than the Great Pyramid in Egypt. In its own way, the Arch is at least as majestic as the Great Pyramid. The Gateway is shaped as an inverted catenary curve, the same shape that a heavy chain will form if suspended between two points. Covered with a sleek skin of stainless steel, the Arch often reflects dazzling bursts of sunlight. In a beautiful display of symmetry, the height of the arch is the same as the distance between the legs at ground level.

Questions

Read the following questions. Circle the letter of the answer you think is correct.

1. "The skyline of St. Louis, Missouri, is fairly unremarkable" is
   a. a fact.
   b. an opinion.

2. Saarinen's winning design was
   a. modeled after other U.S. monuments.
   b. unlike any other monument.
   c. part of a series of monuments.
   d. less expensive to construct than other monuments.

3. The sentence "The Gateway Arch is a masterpiece of engineering, a monument even taller than the Great Pyramid in Egypt" follows which pattern?
   a. fact/fact
   b. fact/opinion
   c. opinion/fact
   d. opinion/opinion

4. The Gateway Arch is shaped like
a. a rainbow.
b. a rectangle.
c. a pyramid.
d. a square.

LESSON SUMMARY

Facts are things that are *known* to be true. **Opinions,** on the other hand, are things that are *believed* to be true. To distinguish between fact and opinion, determine whether the claim is *debatable* or not. If it is debatable, it is probably an opinion. Good writers often support their opinions with facts; this makes their opinions more reasonable. To identify specific facts in a passage, use key words and structure as your guides.

Skill Building until Next Time

1. Listen to what people say today. For example, make a list of statements that are made on a local or national news program. Do the reporters state facts or opinions? When they state opinions, do they support them?

2. Practice turning facts into opinions and opinions into facts. For example, turn the fact "Today is Wednesday" into an opinion, such as "Wednesday is the best day of the week." (Then you could support that opinion by offering support: "Wednesday is the best day of the week because that's when I have music lessons.")

ANSWERS

EXERCISE 1

1. Opinion
2. Opinion
3. Fact
4. Opinion
5. Opinion
6. Opinion
7. Fact
8. Opinion
9. Fact
10. Opinion

EXERCISE 2

1. b. Whether the skyline is "unremarkable" is debatable. It is a matter of opinion.
2. b. The second paragraph states that "the winner of this contest was a plan for a completely different type of structure."
3. c. The first part of the sentence, "The Gateway Arch is a masterpiece of engineering," is an opinion; it makes a judgment about the Arch and is debatable. The second part of the sentence, "a monument even taller than the Great Pyramid in Egypt," is not debatable; it is a matter of fact.
4. a. The exact shape of the Arch is described in the third paragraph. It is an inverted curve and has no angles, so it cannot be a rectangle or a pyramid.

L · E · S · S · O · N

PUTTING IT ALL TOGETHER

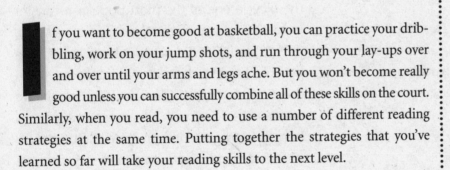

5

SECTION SUMMARY

This lesson reviews what you learned in Lessons 1–4: active reading strategies, finding the main idea, defining words from context, and distinguishing between fact and opinion. In the practice exercise, you'll get to use all of these reading comprehension skills together.

I f you want to become good at basketball, you can practice your dribbling, work on your jump shots, and run through your lay-ups over and over until your arms and legs ache. But you won't become really good unless you can successfully combine all of these skills on the court. Similarly, when you read, you need to use a number of different reading strategies at the same time. Putting together the strategies that you've learned so far will take your reading skills to the next level.

WHAT YOU'VE LEARNED

These are the reading strategies you've learned so far.

Lesson 1: Becoming an Active Reader. You learned that active reading is the key to reading success. Active readers use five specific strategies to understand what they read:

- skimming ahead and jumping back
- highlighting key words and ideas
- looking up unfamiliar vocabulary words
- recording questions and reactions
- looking for clues

Lesson 2: Finding the Main Idea. You learned that the **main idea** is different from the **subject**. The main idea makes an **assertion** about the subject. This idea is **general** enough to hold together all of the ideas in a passage. It is the thought that controls the whole passage, and this thought is often expressed in a **topic sentence**. The other sentences in the passage provide support for the main idea.

Lesson 3: Defining Words from Context. You learned how to figure out what unfamiliar words mean from their **context**—the surrounding words and ideas. You looked for clues in the sentences around the unfamiliar word.

Lesson 4: Distinguishing between Fact and Opinion. You learned that a **fact** is something *known* to be true while an **opinion** is something *believed* to be true. Main ideas are often opinions. Good writers use facts to support their opinions.

If any of these terms or strategies are unfamiliar, STOP. Take some time to review the term or strategy that is unclear.

SECTION 1 PRACTICE

Now it's time to use all of the above skills at once. (This will become more natural as your skills improve.) Read the passage below carefully. If you come across unfamiliar words circle them, but *don't* look them up until *after* you've answered all of the questions. Take as much time as you need and remember to read actively. (The sentences are numbered to make the questions easier to follow.)

Bicycles

(1) Today, bicycles are so common that it's hard to believe they haven't always been around. (2) But two hundred years ago, bicycles didn't even exist, and the first bicycle, invented in Germany in 1818, was nothing like our bicycles today. (3) It was made of wood and didn't even have pedals. (4) Since then, however, numerous innovations and improvements in design have made the bicycle one of the most popular means of recreation and transportation around the world.

(5) In 1839, Kirkpatrick Macmillan, a Scottish blacksmith, dramatically improved upon the original bicycle design. (6) Macmillan's machine had tires with iron rims to keep them from getting worn down. (7) He also used foot-operated cranks similar to pedals so his bicycle could be ridden at a quick pace. (8) It didn't look much like a modern bicycle, though, because its back wheel was substantially larger than its front wheel. (9) In 1861, the French Michaux brothers took the evolution of the bicycle a step further by inventing an improved crank mechanism.

(10) Ten years later, James Starley, an English inventor, revolutionized bicycle design. (11) He made the front wheel many times larger than the back wheel, put a gear on the

pedals to make the bicycle more efficient, and lightened the wheels by using wire spokes. (12) Although this bicycle was much lighter and less tiring to ride, it was still clumsy, extremely top heavy, and ridden mostly for entertainment.

(13) It wasn't until 1874 that the first truly modern bicycle appeared on the scene. (14) Invented by another Englishman, H.J. Lawson, the "safety bicycle" would look familiar to today's cyclists. (15) This bicycle had equal-sized wheels, which made it less prone to toppling over. (16) Lawson also attached a chain to the pedals to drive the rear wheel. (17) With these improvements, the bicycle became extremely popular and useful for transportation. (18) Today they are built, used, and enjoyed all over the world.

Questions

1. Highlight the passage. Which words and ideas should be underlined? _____

_____

_____

2. The main idea of this passage is best expressed in which sentence?
   a. Sentence (1): Today, bicycles are so common that it's hard to believe they haven't always been around.
   b. Sentence (13): It wasn't until 1874 that the first truly modern bicycle appeared on the scene.
   c. Sentence (4): Since then, however, numerous innovations and improvements in design have made the bicycle one of the most popular means of recreation and transportation around the world.
   d. Sentence (18): Today they are built, used, and enjoyed all over the world.

3. Which of the following would be the best title for this passage?
   a. Bicycles Are Better
   b. A Ride through the History of Bicycles
   c. Cycle Your Way to Fitness
   d. The Popularity of Bicycles

4. Which sentence best expresses the main idea of paragraph 3?
   a. Macmillan was a great inventor.
   b. Macmillan's bike didn't look much like our modern bikes.
   c. Macmillan's bike could be ridden quickly.
   d. Macmillan made important changes in bicycle design.

5. An *innovation*, as it is used in Sentence (4), is
   a. a new way of doing something.
   b. a design.
   c. an improvement.
   d. a clever person.

6. *Revolutionized*, as it is used in Sentence (10), most nearly means
   a. cancelled.
   b. changed drastically.
   c. became outdated.
   d. exercised control over.

7. The word *prone*, as it is used in Sentence (15), means
   a. lying down.
   b. unbalanced.
   c. incapable of doing something.
   d. likely to do something.

8. Which of the following sentences from the passage represents the writer's opinion?

   a. Sentence (1)

   b. Sentence (6)

   c. Sentence (9)

   d. Sentence (16)

9. Sentence (8), "It didn't look much like a modern bicycle, though, because its back wheel was substantially larger than its front wheel," follows which pattern?

   a. fact, fact

   b. fact, opinion

   c. opinion, fact

   d. opinion, opinion

10. Macmillan added iron rims to the tires of his bicycle to

   a. add weight to the bicycle.

   b. make the tires last longer.

   c. make the ride less bumpy.

   d. make the ride less tiring.

11. The first person to use a gear system on bicycles was

   a. H. J. Lawson.

   b. Kirkpatrick Macmillan.

   c. The Michaux brothers.

   d. James Starley.

12. Starley's addition of wire spokes made the bicycle

   a. lighter.

   b. less likely to tip over.

   c. more efficient.

   d. safer.

Skill Building until Next Time

1. Review the Skill Building sections from each lesson in this section. Try any Skill Builders you didn't already do.

2. Write a paragraph or two about what you've learned in this section. Begin your paragraph with a clear topic sentence and then write several supporting sentences. Try to use at least one new word you learned this week as you write.

ANSWERS

SECTION 1 PRACTICE

1. The passage should be highlighted or underlined as follows (answers may vary slightly, as you may have highlighted or underlined words or ideas that are particularly interesting to you). Here, we've underlined main ideas and key innovations in bicycle design. We did not underline the effects of these innovations or the problems with these new designs. By highlighting the innovations, though, we can quickly and easily find that related information.

Bicycles

(1) Today, bicycles are so common that it's hard to believe they haven't always been around. (2) But two hundred years ago, bicycles didn't even exist, and <u>the first bicycle, invented</u> in Germany <u>in 1818, was nothing like our bicycles today</u>. (3) It was made of wood and didn't even have pedals. (4) Since then, however, <u>numerous innovations and improvements in design have made the bicycle one of the most popular means of recreation and transportation around the world</u>.

(5) In 1839, Kirkpatrick <u>Macmillan</u>, a Scottish blacksmith, <u>dramatically improved upon the original bicycle design</u>. (6) Macmillan's machine had <u>tires with iron rims</u> to keep them from getting worn down. (7) He also used <u>foot-operated cranks</u> similar to pedals so his bicycle could be ridden at a quick pace. (8) It didn't look much like a modern bicycle, though, because its <u>back wheel was substantially larger than its front</u> wheel. (9) In 1861 the French <u>Michaux brothers</u> took the evolu-tion of the bicycle a step further by invent-ing an <u>improved crank mechanism</u>.

(10) Ten years later, James <u>Starley</u>, an English inventor, <u>revolutionized bicycle design</u>. (11) He made the <u>front wheel many times larger than the back wheel, put a gear on the pedals</u> to make the bicycle more efficient, and lightened the wheels by using <u>wire spokes</u>. (12) Although this bicy-cle was much lighter and less tiring to ride, it was still clumsy, extremely top heavy, and ridden mostly for entertainment.

(13) It wasn't until <u>1874 that the first truly modern bicycle</u> appeared on the scene. (14) Invented by another Englishman, H.J. Law-son, the "safety bicycle" would look famil-iar to today's cyclists. (15) This bicycle had <u>equal-sized wheels</u>, which made it less prone to toppling over. (16) Lawson also attached a <u>chain</u> to the pedals to drive the rear wheel. (17) <u>With these improvements, the bicycle became extremely popular and useful for transportation</u>. (18) Today they are built, used, and enjoyed all over the world.

2. c. This is the only sentence general enough to encompass all of the ideas in the passage. Each paragraph describes the innovations that led to the modern design of the bicycle, and this design has made it popular around the world.

3. b. The essay describes the history of the bicycle, from its invention in 1818 to its modern design.

4. d. Macmillan may have been a great inventor, but this paragraph describes only his innovations in bicycle design. The first sentence in this paragraph expresses this main idea in a clear topic sentence. The rest of the paragraph pro-vides specific examples of the improvements he made in bicycle design.

5. a. An *innovation* is a new way of doing something. The first clue is in Sentence (3), which describes the first bicycle—"it was made of wood and didn't even have pedals." Clearly, bicycles have changed dramatically. Other clues can be found in the following paragraphs, which describe the various changes made to bicycle design. Each bicycle designer came up with a new way of building a bicycle.

6. b. *Revolutionized* means changed drastically. Starley's changes to the bicycle were major changes that enabled the development of the modern bicycle.

7. d. Though *prone* does also mean "lying down," that is not how it is used in this sentence. Here, the context clues tell us that the best answer is "likely to do something." Since Lawson's design was called the "safety bicycle," we can assume it was less likely to tip over because of his innovations.

8. a. Of the four sentences, this is the only one that is debatable.

9. c. The first part of the sentence, "It didn't look much like a modern bicycle," is an opinion; it is debatable. The second part of the sentence, "its back wheel was substantially larger than its front wheel," is a fact.

10. b. Since the question is asking for a specific fact about Macmillan's design, you should know to look in the second paragraph. Then you can find the sentence with the key words "iron rims"—the second sentence—to finding the correct answer. This phrase is easy to find because it's been highlighted.

11. d. If you highlighted the various innovations, then all you have to do is scan the highlighted parts of the passage. Otherwise, you'd have to read through paragraphs 2, 3, and 4 to find the correct answer.

12. a. Again, the question is asking for a specific fact about a specific inventor's design, so you know to go directly to the paragraph about Starley. Then, look for the key words "wire spokes." They should be easy to find because you've highlighted the various innovations.

If You Missed:	Then Study:
Question 1	Lesson 1
Question 2	Lesson 2
Question 3	Lesson 2
Question 4	Lesson 2
Question 5	Lesson 3
Question 6	Lesson 3
Question 7	Lesson 3
Question 8	Lesson 4
Question 9	Lesson 4
Question 10	Lesson 4
Question 11	Lesson 4
Question 12	Lesson 4

S · E · C · T · I · O · N

STRUCTURE

2

Now that you've covered the basics, you can begin to focus on an important reading comprehension strategy: recognizing and understanding structure. How do writers organize their ideas?

Think of a writer as an architect. A building must have a certain number of rooms. But how many rooms there are and how those rooms are arranged is up to the architect. The same goes for a piece of writing. How the sentences and ideas are arranged is entirely up to the writer. Writers must decide which ideas go where and move from one idea to another in an organized way.

Architects generally use one of several basic organizational patterns when they design a building. The same is true for writers when they "design" a text. These basic patterns help writers organize their ideas effectively. In Section 2, you'll study four of those organizational patterns:

- chronological order
- order of importance
- comparing and contrasting similarities and differences
- cause and effect

You'll learn how to recognize these four patterns, and you'll understand why writers use them.

L·E·S·S·O·N

CHRONOLOGICAL ORDER

6

LESSON SUMMARY
This lesson focuses on one of the most basic organizing principles: time. You'll learn how writers organize ideas chronologically, and you'll learn how to recognize this structure.

There are many ways to tell a story. Some stories start in the middle and flash back to the beginning. A few stories actually start at the end and tell the story in reverse. But most of the time, stories start at the beginning, describing what happened first and then what happened next, and next, and so on until the end. When writers tell a story in the order in which things happened, they are using **chronological order**.

KEEPING TRACK OF TIME: TRANSITIONS

Much of what you read is arranged in chronological order. Newspaper and magazine articles, instructions and procedures, and essays about personal experiences usually use this pattern. In fact, several of the passages you've read so far—about Wilma Rudolph, Goran Kropp, and the history of bicycles—use time to organize ideas. First, we learned about Wilma's childhood illnesses, then her struggle to learn to walk again as a teenager, and then her Olympic successes as a young woman. Similarly, we read about Goran Kropp's journey to Mount Everest (first), his ascent up the mountain (second), and his return to Sweden (third). The bicycle passage relates the history of bicycles from their invention in 1818 through several stages of redesign.

Each of these passages provides several clues that they use in chronological order. The bicycle passage guides us by listing the years, so we can see how the design of bicycles progressed through time. The author lists five specific dates—1818, 1839, 1861, 1874 and 1893—and, in the third paragraph, a signal phrase, "Ten years later," which indicates the year 1871. Notice how this works in two of those paragraphs:

In 1839, Kirkpatrick Macmillan, a Scottish blacksmith, dramatically improved upon the original bicycle design. Macmillan's machine had tires with iron rims to keep them from getting worn down. He also used foot-operated cranks similar to pedals so his bicycle could be ridden at a quick pace. It didn't look much like a modern bicycle, though, because its back wheel was substantially larger than its front wheel. In 1861, the French Michaux brothers took the evolution of the bicycle a step further by inventing an improved crank mechanism.

Ten years later, James Starley, an English inventor, revolutionized bicycle design. He made the front wheel many times larger than the back wheel, put a gear on the pedals to make the bicycle more efficient, and lightened the wheels by using wire spokes. Although this bicycle was much lighter and less tiring to ride, it was still clumsy, extremely top heavy, and ridden mostly for entertainment.

These important **transitional words and phrases** guide us through the essay. Because of the transitions, we know exactly when things are happening. We can follow along when the essay shifts from one idea (the Macmillan and Michaux innovations) to another (Starley's innovations). The transitional words keep these events linked together in chronological order.

Transitions are so important that we'd often be lost without them. Imagine, for example, if the bicycle passage didn't have any transitions. Without these dates and transitional phrases, we have no idea of the time frame in which these changes in design took place. Did these changes occur over five years? Ten? A hundred? We wouldn't be able to tell.

Common Transitional Words and Phrases

There are many ways writers signal time order in a chronological passage. Below is a list of some of the most common transitional words and phrases:

afterward	eventually	later	suddenly
as soon as	finally	meanwhile	then
at last	first, second, third	next	when
before, after	immediately	now	while
during	in the meantime	soon	

EXERCISE 1
Questions

Below is a paragraph with all of the transitional words and phrases removed. Read it carefully. Then, choose from the list of transitions below to fill in the blanks and create a smooth, readable paragraph.

It was just one of those days. _____, I woke up half an hour late. _____, _____ rushing to get ready, I realized that the shirt I was wearing had a big stain on it. _____ I quickly changed, grabbed a granola bar and banana for breakfast, and raced out the door. _____, I was standing at the bus stop wondering where my bus could be. _____ I remembered that I was supposed to set my clock back an hour for daylight savings time. _____ I realized I wasn't late—I was a whole hour early!

Transitions

a few minutes later	first	suddenly	then
after	so	that's when	

THE RIGHT SEQUENCE OF EVENTS

Transitions are very important, but even transitions can't do much for a passage if the ideas are all out of order. Imagine, for example, that you were trying to follow a recipe that didn't list the steps in the proper sequence. You'd probably end up ordering pizza for dinner or eating leftovers. If the items aren't in the proper sequence—if you aren't told the correct order for doing things—you're going to have lots of trouble.

The consequences of not following the proper order can be very serious, so it's very important that you be able to recognize sequencing clues. For example, the paragraph below lists five steps that you must follow to participate in a charity walk-a-thon. Read the paragraph carefully and actively, underlining the steps as you read them.

Thank you for your interest in the Mountain View Children's Hospital Charity Walk-a-Thon. In order to participate in the walk, you must first register with the Hospital Development Office (located on the first floor in the West Wing). There you will receive a sponsor sheet and walking guidelines. After you register, you should begin recruiting sponsors immediately. Recruit as many sponsors as possible—the more sponsors, the more funds we can raise for our programs. On the day of the walk, please arrive by 7:30 A.M. Be sure to bring your sponsor sheet and registration information. When you arrive, go immediately to the sign-in desk. Then, proceed to the warm-up area, where you will receive a T-shirt and refreshments. The walk will officially begin at 8:30.

Did you correctly identify the five different steps? We've outlined them below.

1. Register with the Hospital Development Office.
2. Recruit sponsors.
3. Arrive by 7:30 A.M. on the day of the walk-a-thon.
4. Go to the sign-in desk.
5. Go to the warm-up area.

Here's how they appeared in the paragraph. The steps are underlined and the transitions (the clues) are highlighted in bold face.

Thank you for your interest in the Mountain View Children's Hospital Charity Walk-a-Thon.

In order to participate in the walk, you must **first register with the Hospital Development Office** (located on the first floor in the West Wing). There you will receive a sponsor sheet and walking guidelines. **After you register,** you should begin recruiting sponsors immediately. Recruit as many sponsors as possible—the more sponsors, the more funds we can raise for our programs. **On the day of the walk,** please arrive by 7:30 A.M. Be sure to bring your sponsor sheet and registration information. **When you arrive,** go immediately to the sign-in desk. **Then,** proceed to the warm-up area, where you will receive a T-shirt and refreshments. The walk will officially begin at 8:30.

If you miss a step in this process, you may not be able to participate in the walk-a-thon. Thus, it's important that you be able to identify each step and the order in which the steps must be taken.

SEQUENCING CLUES

One of the most obvious and most basic sequencing clues is the numbered list, as in the recipe below. Instead of using numbers, writers may sometimes use the transitions *first, second, third,* and so on to indicate proper order. In addition, there are other ways that writers show the correct sequence of events. For example, read the recipe below carefully and actively:

Briarcliff Blackberry Jam
Yield: 5 cups

    8 cups crushed blackberries
    5 cups sugar
    2 tablespoons lemon juice

1. Mix all ingredients in a Dutch oven.
2. Heat to boiling over high heat, stirring frequently.
3. Boil uncovered, continuing to stir, until the mixture is translucent and thick—about 25 minutes.
4. Quickly skim off foam, as soon as the mixture thickens.
5. Immediately pour jam into hot, sterilized jars, leaving ¼ inch headspace.
6. Seal with canning-jar lids.

Notice how this recipe gives plenty of clues for proper sequencing. First, all of the steps are numbered. Second, the writer provides "carry over clues" that link one step to another. In Step 3, for example, we are told to *continue to stir.* Thus, we can see that there was a previous step—Step 2—in which we were told to stir. In Step 4, we are told to skim off the foam *as soon as the mixture thickens.* Thus, we know that this step must come after Step 3, which tells us to stir "until the mixture is translucent and thick."

EXERCISE 2

The Briarcliff jam recipe includes instructions for sterilizing the jam jars. These steps are listed below in random order. Place them in the proper order by numbering them from 1–7 on the next page. Use the "carry over clues" that link the events together to find the correct sequence. (The first step has been identified to get you started.)

_____ Boil gently and uncovered for 15 minutes.

_____ Place washed jars in a pan with a rack and cover with hot water.

_____ Wash inspected jars in hot, soapy water.

_____ Let jars stand in the hot water until 5 minutes before you are ready to fill with jam.

_1._ Examine the tops and edges of jars and discard any with chips or cracks, because they will prevent an airtight seal.

_____ Remove pan from heat but keep jars in the hot water. Cover.

_____ Heat water in pan to boiling.

LESSON SUMMARY

Chronological order is a very common and useful organizational pattern. Events happen (or should happen) in a certain order, so writers often present them in that sequence. Keep an eye out for transitional words and phrases that signal this type of organization.

Skill Building until Next Time

1. Think about a procedure that you follow regularly, such as brushing your teeth or doing the dishes. Write down the different steps in that procedure. Arrange them in chronological order and include strong transitions so that someone else can follow your directions from start to finish.

2. As you read today, put the events you read about in chronological order. A newspaper article, for example, will often start with the most important information first and then provide some historical background. Revise the order so that everything proceeds chronologically.

ANSWERS

EXERCISE 1

Here's the paragraph with the transitions in place. Your answers may vary slightly:

It was just one of those days. <u>First</u>, I woke up half an hour late. <u>Then</u>, <u>after</u> rushing to get ready, I realized that the shirt I was wearing had a big stain on it. <u>So</u> I quickly changed, grabbed a granola bar and banana for breakfast, and raced out the door. <u>A few minutes later</u>, I was standing at the bus stop wondering where my bus could be. <u>Suddenly</u> I remembered that I was supposed to set my clock back an hour for daylight savings time. <u>That's when</u> I realized I wasn't late—I was a whole hour early!

EXERCISE 2

The correct order is as follows. The sequencing clues are underlined.

1. Examine the tops and edges of jars and discard any with chips or cracks, because they will prevent an airtight seal.
2. Wash <u>inspected jars</u> in hot, soapy water.
3. Place <u>washed jars</u> in a pan with a rack and cover with hot water.
4. Heat water <u>in pan</u> to boiling.
5. <u>Boil</u> gently uncovered for 15 minutes.
6. <u>Remove pan from heat</u> but keep jars in the hot water. Cover.
7. Let jars stand <u>in the hot water</u> until 5 minutes before you are ready to fill with jam.

L·E·S·S·O·N

ORDER OF IMPORTANCE

7

LESSON SUMMARY

Another common organizational pattern is order of importance. This lesson will show you how to recognize this structure so you can identify which ideas are most important in a text. You'll also learn how writers can combine organizational strategies.

t's a scientifically proven fact: People remember beginnings and endings better than middles. In the classroom, for example, you're most likely to remember the topics covered at the beginning and the end of class. Writers have instinctively known this for a long time. That's why many pieces of writing are organized by *order of importance*.

With this organizational pattern, writers use **rank** instead of time as their organizing principle. That is, the first idea a writer describes isn't what *happened* first; it's the idea that's most or least *important*. Writers can start with the most important idea and then work down the line to the least important idea. Or, they can do the opposite: start with the least important idea and build up to the most important.

MOST IMPORTANT TO LEAST IMPORTANT

Both the most-to-least important and least-to-most important organizational patterns use rank as the organizing principle. But they're not exactly interchangeable. Writers will choose one or the other because each of these patterns has a different effect.

Organizing ideas from most important to least important, for example, puts the most essential information *first*. This is often the best approach when writers are offering advice or when they want to be sure readers get the essential information right away. A newspaper article is a good example. News reports generally don't follow chronological order; instead, they begin with the most important information. Writers give us the *who, what, when, where,* and *why* information about the event. Here's an example from a school newspaper article:

Chess Team Wins First Championship!
Yesterday the Oakville High Chess Team won its first state championship in an exciting victory over Winslow High. The team, led by captain Vassil Matic, was losing four matches to three when Magdalena Lukas, a sophomore, won a decisive game against Winslow High captain Julian Mille. Matic then won the tie-breaker to defeat Winslow and bring home the trophy.

This was only the second time the team qualified for the state championship. Two years ago, the team made it to the state championship for the first time but was eliminated during the first round of competitions. The chess team was formed in 1994 by former students Ainsley Pace, Mark Waters, and Shane Trombull. Mr. Trombull is now an advisor for the team.

Notice how this article begins with the most important information: the chess team's victory. Chronologically, this was the *last* event in the series of events described in the article, but here it comes first because it is most important. Next, the article describes the decisive moments in the match—the second most important information. Finally, the article offers some history of the chess club. This information may be interesting, but in terms of the event, it isn't all that important.

Newspaper articles are organized this way for a reason. A newspaper contains so much information that readers rarely read an entire article. In fact, newspaper readers will often read only the first few paragraphs of an article and skim—or skip—the rest. Therefore, it's essential to get the most important information across at the very beginning.

Other texts use this strategy for similar reasons. They want readers to know right from the start what's most important. If you are reading a passage about ways to improve your study skills, for example, you're not likely to read much of the text if you don't find the first tip or two to be very useful. Besides, writers will want to be sure you get the most important information. The best way to do that is to put it first.

EXERCISE 1

Below is a passage about safety on the Internet. Read it carefully and actively. Then write the answers on the lines that follow.

Net Safety
Though it may seem like cyberspace is a pretty safe place, in reality, the Internet poses some very real dangers for teens. To be safe when you're online, follow these guidelines. First and foremost, **protect your privacy. Never** give your real last name, address, or telephone number to anyone. Second, **never** agree to meet with someone you've talked with on the Internet without asking permission from your parents

first. Third, remember that **people are not always what they seem.** Someone who is very nice to you online could turn out to be someone eager to hurt you in person. Finally, **trust your instincts.** If someone uses bad language or mentions things that make you uncomfortable, don't respond and log off. If you come across a site where the content makes you uncomfortable, exit it as quickly as possible.

Questions

1. According to this passage, what's the most important thing you can do to be safe on the Internet?

   _____

   _____

2. What is the second most important thing?_____

   _____

   _____

3. What is the third most important thing?_____

   _____

   _____

4. What is the fourth most important thing?_____

   _____

   _____

TRANSITIONS

Here's a list of the most common transitions writers apply when using the order of importance organizational pattern. Most of these phrases work for both most-to-least important and least-to-most important patterns:

above all	first, second, third	more importantly	most importantly
first and foremost	last but not least	moreover	

LEAST IMPORTANT TO MOST IMPORTANT

Sometimes instead of *starting* with the most important idea, writers prefer to *end* with the most important idea. Not only does this leave readers with a strong concluding impression, but also it takes advantage of the "snowball effect." The snowball effect is the "build up" or force that a writer gets from starting with what's least important and moving toward what's most important. Like the layers of snow in a snowball, the writer's ideas build upon one another, getting bigger and stronger as they become increasingly important. By starting with the least impor-

tant point, writers can also create suspense, since the reader has to wait for the final and most important idea.

USING LEAST-TO-MOST FOR ARGUMENTS

Writers often use the least-to-most important structure when they are presenting an **argument.** That's because this kind of structure is more convincing than a most-to-least organization. The more controversial the argument, the more important this structure. In an argument, you need to build your case piece by piece and win your readers over point by point. If your less important points make sense to the reader, then your more important points will come off stronger. And, as the saying goes, writers often "save the best for last" because that's where "the best" often has the most impact.

In other words, the writer's **purpose** for writing helps determine the organizational pattern he or she uses. In turn, the structure influences how you take in and understand what you read.

Take a look at the following student essay, for example. Notice how the writer builds her case, piece-by-piece, saving her strongest and most important point for last. As you read, mark up the text by underlining her main idea and her key supporting points.

Make Us Volunteers!

There's been a proposal to add a new requirement to the eighth grade curriculum: 10 hours of volunteer work each quarter. Students would not be able to graduate to ninth grade without 40 hours of volunteer work on their records. Some will argue that this is forced volunteerism, and therefore not volunteerism at all. But I think that's beside the point. What matters is that students will benefit enormously from such a program.

For one thing, volunteer work is a confidence booster. When you help someone else, when you make someone else feel good, it makes you feel better about yourself. And who couldn't benefit from that? Students will go through the year knowing that they are helping others and making a difference in their community. They will know that *they* have the power to make people's lives better.

More importantly, volunteering will help students become more compassionate and tolerant. They will see that there are all kinds of people in the world with all kinds of problems. But underneath those problems, they're still people just like you and me.

But the most important benefit of this program is that it will teach students that they have a responsibility to other people. We have a *duty* to help others whenever we can. Students will learn that other people are counting on them to meet very real and important needs. They will learn that when they fail to fulfill their responsibilities, they may hurt other human beings. They will learn that when they make a commitment, it is important to honor it.

What is the writer's main idea? Did you identify it as the idea stated in the last sentence of the first paragraph—that "students will benefit enormously from this program"? Good. Next, did you correctly identify her three supporting ideas? They're listed below:

- Volunteering will boost students' confidence.
- Volunteering will help students become more compassionate and tolerant.
- Volunteering will teach students that they have a responsibility to others.

These points are listed from least important to most important. The transitions are our biggest clues to this structure. Here are the transitions in the order in which they're used:

- for one thing
- more importantly
- but the most important benefit

This structure works well for this argument. The first point is difficult to disagree with; we all know how good it feels to help someone else, and few people would resist this idea. The second point is a little more complicated and controversial. Some readers might be hesitant about working with people they feel are "different." The third point is the one the author thinks is most important, and it's also perhaps the most controversial. Some people would argue that we are *not* duty bound to help others. But this point is easier to accept if we've already accepted the writer's previous two points.

EXERCISE 2

Look at the following list of reasons to read more often. If you were to put these reasons together in a paragraph to convince readers that they should read more, how would you organize the reasons? Rank these reasons first in order of importance and then in the order in which you would present them.

Five Reasons to Read More Often

- It will improve your vocabulary.
- It will improve your reading comprehension.
- It will increase your reading speed.
- It will broaden your understanding of yourself and others.
- It will introduce you to new information and new ideas.

Order of Importance to You

1. _____

2. _____

3. _____

4. _____

5. _____

Order of Presentation

1. _____

2. _____

3. _____

4. _____

5. _____

EXERCISE 3

MOST-TO-LEAST IMPORTANT

There are many benefits to reading more often. First and foremost, reading more will broaden your understanding of yourself and of other people. It will also introduce you to new information and ideas. Furthermore, it will improve your overall reading comprehension so you'll begin to understand more of what you read. In addition, reading more will improve your vocabulary and increase your reading speed.

LEAST-TO-MOST IMPORTANT

Reading more often can benefit you in many ways. First of all, it will increase your reading speed, so that you can read more in less time. Second, it will improve your vocabulary. Third, it will improve your overall reading comprehension, and you'll understand more of what you read. In addition, reading more will introduce you to new information and ideas. Most importantly, reading will broaden your understanding of yourself and other people.

Questions

1. Underline and write down the transitional words and phrases in the examples above. _____

   _____

   _____

2. Underline and write down the topic sentence in each paragraph._____

   _____

   _____

LESSON SUMMARY

Order of importance is an organizational strategy you will see often. Writers may move from most important to least important or from least important to most important. The order writers choose depends upon their purposes. Arguments usually run from least-to-most important. Newspaper articles and other factual texts often use the most-to-least approach. This structure helps you see the writer's purpose so you can better understand what you read.

Skill Building until Next Time

1. You probably see many lists throughout the day, such as to-do lists and shopping lists. Notice how these lists are organized. Are the items listed by order of importance? If so, are they listed from least to most important or from most to least? If the items are not organized by rank, list them in order of importance.

2. Listen carefully to a commercial on television. Notice how the ideas are presented. If advertisers are trying to convince you of something, how do they organize their ideas? If they are giving advice, are their ideas organized in a different way?

ANSWERS

EXERCISE 1

1. Protect your privacy: Don't give out your name, address or phone number.
2. Never agree to meet someone you met online without your parents' permission.
3. Remember that people are not always what they seem.
4. Trust your instincts.

Notice that this passage uses the *first, second, third* transitions we saw in the last lesson on chronological order. Here, however, these transitions don't indicate a *sequence* of doing things; rather, they indicate the *rank* of these safety suggestions.

EXERCISE 2

In which order did you choose to present your ideas? Most important to least important? Or least to most? Either structure will work beautifully with these ideas. You may want to hit your readers with what's most important from the start so that you make sure you catch their attention. Or you may want to save your best ideas for last so that you build up to what's most important. Below are two examples of how you might have written your paragraph. One version uses least-to-most important, the other most-to-least important. Notice the clear topic sentence and strong transitions in both examples.

EXERCISE 3

1. In the most-to-least important paragraph, the transitions are *first and foremost, also, furthermore,* and *in addition.* In the least-to-most paragraph, the transitions are *first of all, second, third, in addition,* and *most importantly.*
2. In both paragraphs, the first sentence is the topic sentence, which expresses the main idea.

L·E·S·S·O·N

SIMILARITIES AND DIFFERENCES: COMPARISON AND CONTRAST

8

LESSON SUMMARY

This lesson explores another organizational pattern writers often use: comparing and contrasting similarities and differences.

magine for a moment that an alien landed in your backyard. How would you describe this alien to your friends? Chances are you'd rely heavily on **comparison** and **contrast.** You might say, for example, that the alien looked a lot like an octopus (comparison), except that it had twelve tentacles instead of just eight (contrast). Or you might say the alien looked *exactly* like the alien in the movie *E.T.* (comparison) only about ten times as large (contrast).

When you show how two or more things are similar, you are **comparing** them. When you show how two or more things are different, you are **contrasting** them. This technique gives you a way to classify or judge the items you're analyzing. By placing two (or more) items side by side, for example, you can see how they measure up against each other. How are they similar or different? And why does it matter? For example, you might say that the film *Crouching Tiger, Hidden Dragon* was even better than *Star Wars*. Both featured warriors with special powers and a love story (comparison). But in *Crouching Tiger*, the fighters relied much more on their physical strength and agility than on automatic weapons, which are plentiful in *Star Wars* (contrast).

And *Crouching Tiger* featured female warriors as strong as (or even stronger than) the male fighters (contrast).

MAIN IDEA IN COMPARISON AND CONTRAST

In writing, whenever an author is comparing and contrasting two or more items, he or she is doing it for a reason. There's something the author wants to point out by putting these two items side by side for analysis. This reason or point is the main idea, which is often stated in a topic sentence. For example, let's take another look at a more developed *Crouching Tiger, Hidden Dragon* and *Star Wars* comparison and contrast:

> Two of the best films ever made are *Star Wars* and *Crouching Tiger, Hidden Dragon.* I've seen both movies at least a dozen times, and as soon as *Crouching Tiger* comes out on video, you can be sure it will be in my collection. While I always will be a loyal *Star Wars* fan, I do have to say that *Crouching Tiger* is an even better film.
>
> Both films feature warriors with special powers. In *Star Wars,* Luke Skywalker, a Jedi knight, has "the force"—a special energy that he can channel to help him overcome evil. Similarly, in *Crouching Tiger,* Li Mu Bai, Yu Shu Lien, and Jen all have special powers that they've developed through rigorous martial arts training. But the characters in *Star Wars* rely heavily on automatic weapons. The warriors in *Crouching Tiger,* in contrast, do all of their fighting with "old-fashioned" weapons such as swords and the most old-fashioned weapon of all—their bodies. What they're able to do with their bodies is much more impressive than anything Luke Skywalker can do with his light saber.

Right from the beginning of this passage, the author's main idea is clear. The writer wants to compare and contrast these two films to show that they're both great, but that *Crouching Tiger* is even better. This idea is stated clearly in the last sentence of the first paragraph (a good example of a topic sentence). Then, the second paragraph looks at one aspect of both films—that they both feature warriors with special powers. After this comparison, the writer shows how they are different within this similarity. It's a nice, strong paragraph because it provides specific evidence for the overall main idea. It also states its own main idea clearly in the last sentence: "What they're able to do with their bodies is much more impressive than anything Luke Skywalker can do with his light saber."

EXERCISE 1

Below is a more complete comparison and contrast of *Star Wars* and *Crouching Tiger, Hidden Dragon.* Read the passage carefully and actively, noting how each paragraph provides support for the overall main idea. Then answer the questions that follow.

The Best of the Best

Two of the best films ever made are *Star Wars* and *Crouching Tiger, Hidden Dragon.* I've seen both movies at least a dozen times, and as soon as *Crouching Tiger* comes out on video, you can be sure it will be in my collection. While I always will be a loyal *Star Wars* fan, I do have to say that *Crouching Tiger* is an even better film.

Both films feature warriors with special powers. In *Star Wars,* Luke Skywalker, a Jedi knight, has "the force"—a special energy that he can channel to help him overcome evil. Similarly, in *Crouching Tiger,* Li Mu Bai, Yu Shu Lien, and Jen all have special powers that they've developed through rigorous martial arts training. But the characters in *Star Wars* rely heavily on automatic weapons. The warriors in *Crouching Tiger,* in contrast, do all of their fighting with "old-fashioned" weapons such as swords and the most old-fashioned weapon of all—their bodies. What they're able to do with their bodies is much more impressive than anything Luke Skywalker can do with his light saber.

More importantly, *Crouching Tiger* gives equal treatment to both sexes. In *Star Wars,* though Princess Leia can (and does) fight, she still relies mostly on the men to fight and save her. In *Crouching Tiger,* however, the female warriors are every bit as strong as the male warriors and do all of the fighting on their own. Shu Lien, Jen, and another woman, Jade Fox, actually do most of the fighting in the movie and defeat many men throughout the film.

The best thing about *Crouching Tiger,* though, is the story of Jen. While *Star Wars* is a great story about good forces against evil forces, *Crouching Tiger* is a great story about a personal rebellion that all young people can relate to. Jen rebels against the society that is going to force her to marry. Who wants to be told whom to love? She rejects being forced into this relationship and runs off. She doesn't know how to handle her strength, though, and is so independent that she even rejects the chance to be Mu Bai's student. Under his guidance, Jen could have become an even greater warrior. But Jen is too independent, and she unintentionally helps to bring about Mu Bai's death and her own. Jen's story shows us that we have a right to determine the course of our lives, but that we also need the guidance of our elders.

Questions

1. What is the similarity discussed in paragraph 3?

_____

_____

2. What is the difference discussed in paragraph 3?

_____

_____

3. What is the similarity discussed in paragraph 4?

_____

_____

4. What is the difference discussed in paragraph 4?

_____

_____

5. What is the main idea of paragraph 4?_____

_____

_____

MULTIPLE STRATEGIES

Organizational patterns are a bit like main ideas. While there is usually one **overall organizing principle** (as there is one overall main idea), there can be other organizing principles in each paragraph (like the main ideas that hold each paragraph together). There can even be two different organizational patterns *working together* in the same paragraph. For example, the *Star Wars/Crouching Tiger* passage uses comparison and contrast as its main organizing principle. But it also uses another strategy to organize the characteristics it compares. Notice how the transitions give this secondary structure away:

paragraph 2: Both films feature . . .

paragraph 3: More importantly . . .

paragraph 4: The best thing about *Crouching Tiger,* though . . .

If you didn't notice it before, it should be clear now that this comparison and contrast also uses order of importance (least-to-most) to organize its ideas.

TRANSITIONS

One of the keys to a good comparison and contrast is strong transitions. It's important to let readers know when you're comparing and when you're contrasting. As a reader, it's important to watch for these transitions.

Here are some words and phrases that show similarity:

and	in a like manner	like
also	in the same way	likewise
both	just as	similarly

The following words and phrases, on the other hand, show difference:

but	in contrast	unlike
conversely	on the contrary	while
however	on the other hand	yet

Notice, for example, how the writer uses transitions in one of the paragraphs comparing *Star Wars* and *Crouching Tiger:*

Both films feature warriors with special powers. In *Star Wars,* Luke Skywalker, a Jedi knight, has "the force"—a special energy that he can channel to help him overcome evil. **Similarly,** in *Crouching Tiger,* Li Mu Bai, Yu Shu Lien, and Jen all have special powers that they've developed through rigorous martial arts training. **But** the characters in *Star Wars* rely heavily on automatic weapons. The warriors in *Crouching Tiger,* **in contrast,** do all of their fighting with "old-fashioned" weapons such as swords and the most old-fashioned weapon of all—their bodies. What they're able to do with their bodies is much more impressive than anything Luke Skywalker can do with his light saber.

STRUCTURE IN COMPARISON AND CONTRAST

We've seen how comparing and contrasting works to support a main idea, and we've looked at how a comparison and contrast uses transitions. Now it's time to look at the comparison and contrast structure.

THE POINT-BY-POINT TECHNIQUE

Comparison and contrast passages are usually organized one of two ways: the point-by-point or block technique. Take a look at the following paragraph, for example:

I'm the oldest of five kids. Yesterday, my youngest sister said she wished she was the oldest. Ha! Let me tell you, being the youngest is better any day. For one thing, the oldest has tons of responsibility. What about the youngest? None. My sis simply has to be there. She doesn't have to do chores, watch the other kids, or help make dinner. For another, the oldest has to "break in" the parents. Since I was the first, my parents had to learn how to be parents—and if they made mistakes, well, I was the one who suffered. Lucky Emily has parents who've already been through this four times. Unlike me, she has parents who are already "well trained."

Notice how this paragraph first states the main idea—"being the youngest is better any day"—and then supports this idea point by point. That is, each time the writer makes a point about what it's like to be oldest, he counters with a point about what it's like to be youngest. Thus, the structure is as follows:

<u>Topic sentence:</u>   youngest is better than oldest
<u>Characteristic one:</u> responsibility (oldest, youngest)
<u>Characteristic two:</u> parents' experience raising children (oldest, youngest)

For each characteristic, the writer directly compares or contrasts A (oldest) and B (youngest). A point-by-point passage, then, uses an AB, AB, AB structure. Then, the writer moves on to the next characteristic and compares or contrasts A and B again.

THE BLOCK TECHNIQUE

The block technique, on the other hand, discusses all of the characteristics of A and *then* discusses all of the characteristics of B. That's why it's called the "block" technique; we get a "block" of text about one item that's being compared and then get a "block" of text about the other item. Here's our previous example rewritten with the block comparison and contrast structure:

I'm the oldest of five kids. Yesterday, my youngest sister said she wished she was the oldest. Ha! Let me tell you, being the youngest is better any day. For one thing, the oldest has tons of responsibility. I always have to do chores, watch the other kids, and help make dinner. For another, the oldest has to "break in" the parents. Since I was the first, my parents had

to learn how to be parents—and if they made mistakes, well, I was the one who suffered. What about the youngest? What kind of responsibility does my sister have? None. My sis simply has to be there. Lucky Emily also has parents who've already been through this four times. Unlike me, she has parents who are already "well trained."

Here, we have an AA, BB structure—first both of the characteristics of being the oldest, then both of the characteristics of being the youngest.

COMPARING AND CONTRASTING MATCHING ITEMS

Though these two youngest/oldest child comparison and contrast passages use two different organizational techniques, they do have one very important thing in common. In both cases, the *characteristics are comparable*. When the writer makes a point about A, she also makes a point about *the same characteristic* in B. She's talking about the same issues for both—responsibility and parent experience. Look what happens when the characteristics aren't comparable:

I'm the oldest of five kids. Yesterday, my youngest sister said she wished she was the oldest. Ha! Let me tell you, being the youngest is better any day. For one thing, the oldest has tons of responsibility. I have to do chores, watch the other kids, and help make dinner. My sister, on the other hand, is always getting her way. Whatever she wants, she gets, from the latest Barbie accessory to tacos for dinner.

This version has a major problem: the two characteristics the writer wishes to compare *aren't the same.* Responsibility and the ability to get one's way are two entirely different issues. As a result, the writer is not really proving the point he makes in the topic sentence. We can't see, from this comparison, that the youngest sister doesn't have the same amount of responsibility or that she doesn't also always get her way.

EXERCISE 2

Suppose you wanted to compare or contrast readers (Item A) to detectives (Item B). Following are five characteristics of being a reader and five characteristics of being a detective. Only *three* characteristics in each list match.

Questions

Find the matching characteristics and draw a line between the columns to connect them. Label whether the characteristics are similarities or differences.

Readers (Item A)

1. Look for clues to understand meaning.

2. Have many different types of books to read.

3. Can choose what book to read.

4. Build their vocabulary by reading.

5. Become better readers with each book.

Detectives (Item B)

1. Have a dangerous job.

2. Get better at solving crimes with each case.

3. Require lots of training.

4. Don't get to choose which cases to work on.

5. Look for clues to solve the crime.

EXERCISE 3

Now that you've matched comparable characteristics, write a short comparison and contrast paragraph below. Make sure you have a clear main idea and use strong transitions.

_____

_____

_____

_____

_____

_____

_____

_____

LESSON SUMMARY

Writers use the comparison and contrast structure to show how two things are alike and how they are different. Look for topic sentences that show the writer's focus (main idea). Watch for transitions, too, that signal comparison or contrast. A comparison and contrast passage may be organized point-by-point or in blocks. In either case, the characteristics should be comparable.

Skill Building until Next Time

1. Today, compare and contrast things around you. For example, you might compare and contrast this year's English class with last year's, or compare and contrast two sports, like football and soccer (you'll have a better comparison if you compare two *team* sports or two *individual* sports rather than comparing a team sport with an individual sport). How are these two things alike? How are they different? Make sure all of the characteristics you choose are comparable. For example, if you compare and contrast football and soccer, you might consider the way the ball is handled, the way goals/points are earned, and the danger level of each sport.

2. As you make these comparisons, try arranging them in both the point-by-point and block structures.

ANSWERS

EXERCISE 1

1. In both movies, the female characters can and do fight.
2. In *Crouching Tiger*, the women don't rely on men at all—they fight for themselves.
3. They're both great stories.
4. They're different kinds of stories. In *Crouching Tiger*, the story is one all young people can relate to.
5. The main idea of paragraph 4 is stated in the first sentence: "The best thing about *Crouching Tiger*, though, is the story of Jen."

EXERCISE 2

Reader 1 corresponds with Detective 5 (similarity).
Reader 3 corresponds with Detective 4 (difference).
Reader 5 corresponds with Detective 2 (similarity)

EXERCISE 3

Answers will vary slightly. Here's one possibility (the transitions are in boldface type):

You may not realize it, but readers are a lot like detectives. An important part of both jobs is looking for clues. **Just as** a detective looks for clues to solve a crime, a reader looks for clues to solve the "mystery" of a text (its meaning). **Another similarity** is that **both** readers and detectives get better at their jobs with practice. A reader gets better at reading comprehension with each book. **Likewise,** a detective becomes better at solving crimes with each case. **One difference, however,** is that while readers get to choose which books they want to read, a detective doesn't have much choice about which case he or she has to work on.

L·E·S·S·O·N
CAUSE AND EFFECT
9

LESSON SUMMARY

"One thing leads to another"—that's the principle behind cause and effect. This lesson explains these two important concepts. You'll learn how to tell the difference between cause and effect, how they're related, and how to judge opinions about cause and effect.

Much of what you read is an attempt to explain either the cause of some action or its effect. For example, an author might try to explain the causes of global warming or the effects of a diet with too much sugar. Or an author might explore the reasons behind a change in school policy or the effects that an injury had on an athlete. As you might expect, authors describing cause and effect often use one of a few general patterns to organize their ideas.

DISTINGUISHING BETWEEN CAUSE AND EFFECT

"For every action," said the famous scientist Sir Isaac Newton, "there is an equal and opposite reaction." Every action results in another action (a *reaction*). Or, in other words, for every action, there is an *effect* caused by that action. Likewise, each action is *caused* by a previous action. In other words, each action has a **cause**—something that made it happen—and an **effect**—something that *it* makes happen. Cause and effect, then, work together; you can't have one without the other. That's why it's very important to be able to distinguish between the two.

> **Cause:** a person or thing that makes something happen or creates an effect
>
> **Effect:** a change created by an action or cause

A passage about **cause** explains *why* something took place. You might ask, for example: Why did Elaine decide to quit the basketball team?

A passage about **effect,** on the other hand, explains *what happened after* something took place. What happened as a result of Elaine's decision? How did it affect the team? How did it affect Elaine?

Thus, we might identify a cause and effect from the previous example as follows:

> Because Elaine quit the team, she was able to join the Drama Club.

What happened? Elaine quit the team (the cause). What was the result? She was able to join the Drama Club (the effect).

EXERCISE 1
Questions

To help you distinguish between cause and effect, try this exercise. Read the sentences below carefully and identify which is the cause and which is the effect in each sentence.

Example: Robin got 10 points taken off his grade because he handed his paper in late.

Cause: Robin handed in his paper late.
Effect: Robin got 10 points taken off his grade.

1. This new detergent has caused a rash on my arms.

   Cause: _____

   Effect: _____

2. Since I joined the track team, I've made a lot of new friends.

   Cause: _____

   Effect: _____

3. I realized that the rash on my arms wasn't created by the new detergent, but by my allergy to wool.

   Cause: _____

   Effect: _____

4. As a result of the new volunteer program, I spend every Thursday night helping in the local soup kitchen.

   Cause: _____

   Effect: _____

5. Because I help feed the homeless, I feel really good about myself.

   Cause: _____

   Effect: _____

TRANSITIONS AND OTHER CLUES

You probably had a lot of success with Practice 1 because of the clues the writers left for you. Just as certain key words indicate whether you're comparing or contrasting, other key words indicate whether things are causes or effects. Here is a partial list of these important clues.

Words Indicating Cause
because (of)   created (by)
caused (by)   since

Words Indicating Effect
as a result   since
consequently   so
hence   therefore

EXERCISE 2
Questions
Reread the sentences in Practice 1. Are there any signal phrases that indicate cause or effect? If so, underline them.

CHAIN REACTIONS

The difference between cause and effect may seem clear, but it's not always easy to separate the two. For one thing, the two work very closely together. For another, effects often *become causes* for other events. Here's an example.

Imagine that you lost your house keys (cause). As a result, you might have to stay in the school library until one of your parents could pick you up (effect). But that *effect* could then *cause* another event. That is, getting stuck in the library might give you two hours of uninterrupted time to get started on your research paper assignment. And *that* might mean that you could go to the baseball game this weekend instead of doing research. Thus, A caused B, B caused C, and C caused D.

A causes → B effect (becomes) cause
→ C effect (becomes) cause → D effect

Effects, then, often become causes for other effects. So one event could be described as either a cause *or* an

effect. It's often important to be able to tell which stage the writer is talking about.

Here's an example of a short chain of cause and effect. Read the passage below carefully and actively. Notice the clues that indicate cause and effect. Underline these transitions as you read.

Yesterday my mother told me I was grounded for life. I was supposed to pick up my sister from her playdate at Ellie's house at 4:00. But I was playing JudoMaster-Extreme at Charlie's house, and I'd actually made it to the fourth level for the first time. So I decided to keep playing. I figured Rosie would enjoy the extra playtime. But Ellie's mom had an appointment and couldn't leave until someone picked up Rosie. She had to call my mom, who had to leave an important meeting to get Rosie.

Notice that this paragraph's purpose is to explain *why* the narrator was grounded for life. This idea is expressed in the topic sentence that begins the paragraph. This sentence reveals that this passage will explain *cause*. But the paragraph talks about *several* different causes. And it also talks about *several* different effects.

Like most events, the narrator's trouble wasn't caused by just *one* thing. Instead, it was caused by a *series* of actions and reactions—a chain of cause and effect. This particular chain began when the narrator reached the fourth level in JudoMaster. Because of that, he decided to keep playing instead of picking up his sister as he was supposed to do.

EXERCISE 3
Questions
There are three other sets of cause and effect in the passage above. What are they? List them below. The first link in the chain is provided to get you started.

Cause 1: He reached the fourth level.

Effect 1: He decided not to get Rosie on time.

Cause 2: He decided not to get Rosie on time.

Effect 2: _____

Cause 3: _____

Effect 3: _____

Cause 4: _____

Effect 4: _____

WHEN ONE CAUSE HAS SEVERAL EFFECTS

Sometimes one cause may have several effects. That is, several things may happen as a result of one action. For example, imagine you lie to a close friend and tell her you can't come over on Friday night because you are grounded—but the truth is that you have another friend coming over. This action could actually create several distinct effects:

1. You might feel pretty guilty for lying.
2. You'd have to make sure you stay home on Friday in case your friend calls.
3. You'd have to make sure your other friend is quiet if your friend calls.
4. You'd have to make sure no one in your family mentions your other friend's visit.

WHEN ONE EFFECT HAS SEVERAL CAUSES

While one cause can have several effects, one effect can also have several causes. For example, read the paragraph below carefully:

Yesterday my mother told me I was grounded for at least a month. I need to be more responsible and get myself together, she said, and I guess she's right. For one thing, I haven't cleaned my room in over a month—and trust me when

I tell you, it's a disaster. And I admit I haven't been doing my other chores around the house. She's also mad because my grades slipped last semester—my A's slid into B's and my B's into C's. We both know I can do better. And she's right—I've been pretty disrespectful to everyone in my family for the past couple of weeks.

Here, the narrator probably wouldn't have been grounded for a month if he'd only done *one* thing wrong. But we can see from this paragraph that there were actually four different causes leading to his being grounded. These aren't causes in a chain of cause and effect; each cause individually *contributed* to this result.

EXERCISE 4
Questions
List the four separate reasons (causes) that the narrator was grounded.

1. _____

2. _____

3. _____

4. _____

OPINIONS ABOUT CAUSE AND EFFECT

Sometimes, a writer will offer his or her *opinion* about why something happened when the facts of the cause(s) aren't clear. Or a writer may predict what he or she thinks will happen because of a certain event (its effects). If this is the case, you need to consider how reasonable those opinions are. Are the writer's ideas logical? Does the writer offer support for the conclusions he or she offers?

A good example is the extinction of the dinosaurs. There have been many proposed causes, such as an asteroid, a devastating disease, even an attack by aliens. For each argument, you'd have to consider the evidence that the writer offers. Does the writer's evidence support the claim that *that* particular cause led to their extinction?

Similarly, imagine your school board was considering a proposal to require students to wear uniforms. In this case, writers might offer their opinion about possible effects of such a policy. Again, you'd have to consider what kind of evidence the writers offered to support their opinions. Take a look at the two paragraphs below, for example:

Paragraph A

The proposal to require public school students to wear uniforms is a bad idea. Can you imagine what it would be like? Everyone will look the same. We'll walk around school like a bunch of zombies in a bad horror movie. Teachers won't even be able to tell us apart. Our personalities will be hidden by the clothes. We will never be able to express ourselves through what we wear. The school will have to have uniform police to make sure everyone is alike.

Paragraph B

I disagree with the proposal to require public school students to wear uniforms. The intentions may be good, but the results will be bad. We should be encouraging individuality. But a uniform policy will tell students that individuality doesn't matter. After all, the way we dress is an important way we express who we are. Worse, the uniform policy will tell kids that conformity is the rule, and if they don't conform, they'll be punished. Kids who don't abide by the uniform dress code will be suspended. Are clothes more important than education?

Both authors predict certain effects of a school uniform policy. You may not agree with either author, but you should be able to see that the second paragraph is much more reasonable than the first. Most of the predicted results in the first paragraph are *not* very likely to happen. They're exaggerated and not supported by facts. The second paragraph, however, offers some support for its predictions. In addition, the predicted results are much more reasonable and therefore much more acceptable.

EXERCISE 5
Questions

Imagine that a not-so-close friend has just offered you a cigarette. In a short paragraph, explain to your friend some of the negative effects that result from smoking.

_____

_____

_____

_____

_____

_____

_____

_____

_____

LESSON SUMMARY

Understanding cause and effect is important for reading success. All events have at least one cause (what made it happen) and at least one effect (the result of what happened). Some events have more than one cause, and some causes have more than one effect. An event is also often part of a chain of cause and effect. Causes and effects are usually signaled by important transitional words and phrases.

Skill Building until Next Time

1. Consider the effects of a recent change in your home, school, or neighborhood. For example, imagine that a new movie theater is being built a few blocks away from your home. How will that affect traffic on your street? How will it affect your own and your family's leisure time? How will it affect the level of noise in your area at night?

2. Consider recent events at home or school. What might have caused them? For example, imagine that your hockey team has been losing a lot of games lately. What might be causing this slump?

ANSWERS

EXERCISE 1

1. Cause: The new detergent.
   Effect: A rash on my arms.
2. Cause: Joining the track team.
   Effect: I made a lot of new friends.
3. Cause: My allergy to wool.
   Effect: A rash on my arms.
4. Cause: The new volunteer program.
   Effect: I spend every Thursday night helping in the local soup kitchen.
5. Cause: I help feed the homeless.
   Effect: I feel really good about myself.

EXERCISE 2

The signal phrases are underlined below.

1. This new detergent <u>has caused</u> a rash on my arms.
2. <u>Since</u> I joined the track team, I've made a lot of new friends.
3. I realized that the rash on my arms wasn't <u>created</u> by the new detergent but by my allergy to wool.
4. <u>As a result</u> of the new volunteer program, I spend every Thursday night helping in the local soup kitchen.
5. <u>Because</u> I help feed the homeless, I feel really good about myself.

EXERCISE 3

Cause 2: He decided not to get Rosie on time.
Effect 2: Ellie's mom couldn't leave for her appointment.

Cause 3: Ellie's mom couldn't leave for her appointment.
Effect 3: She called Rosie's mom.

Cause 4: She called Rosie's mom.
Effect 4: Rosie's mom had to leave a big meeting.

EXERCISE 4

1. He hasn't cleaned his room in more than a month.
2. He hasn't done his other household chores.
3. His grades have slipped.
4. He has been disrespectful to his family.

EXERCISE 5

Answers will vary. Here's one possibility.

No thanks. Do you know how bad cigarettes are for you? First of all, the nicotine in cigarettes is addictive, and could cause you to become addicted to smoking. Smoking is also known to cause lung cancer and cancer of the mouth and throat. And don't forget that smoking will make your clothes and breath smell!

PUTTING IT ALL TOGETHER

SECTION SUMMARY

This lesson pulls together what you've learned about structure in Lessons 6–9. It also gives you more practice in the basics from Lessons 1–4.

Like architects designing a building, writers need a plan for how they will organize their ideas. In the last lesson, you learned four organizational strategies that writers use: arranging ideas according to time, order of importance, similarities and differences, and cause and effect. Now it's time to review these strategies and combine them with the basics you learned in Section 1.

WHAT YOU'VE LEARNED

Here's a quick review of each lesson about structure.

Lesson 6: Chronological Order. You learned that ideas are often presented in chronological order—the order in which they occurred or should occur. Proper sequencing is important and writers often provide lots of clues through transitions.

Lesson 7: Order of Importance. You also learned that ideas can be organized by rank. They can begin with the most important idea and work to the least important idea, or vice versa, from the least important to the most important. The "least-to-most" structure is most often used in persuasive writing.

Lesson 8: Similarities and Differences; Comparison and Contrast. You saw how ideas are arranged by similarities and differences. Writers match corresponding features of A and B and show how they are alike or different. Ideas can be presented either point by point or in blocks.

Lesson 9: Cause and Effect. Here, ideas are organized so that readers can see what caused an event to take place or what effect(s) an event had. Sometimes writers describe a chain of cause and effect as well as multiple causes and multiple effects.

If any of these terms or strategies are unfamiliar, STOP. Take some time to review the term or strategy that is unclear.

SECTION 2 PRACTICE

Although writers often have one overall organizing principle, they often combine two or more organizational strategies as they write. Keep this in mind as you read through the practice passages below. As you read, look for clues to determine the overall structure and watch for

smaller sections that organize ideas in a different way *within* the main structure. Read each passage actively and carefully. Then answer the questions that follow.

EXERCISE 1

(1) Too much sun can be deadly. (2) First of all, too much sun can dry your skin, which in turn reduces its elasticity and speeds up the aging process. (3) Second, too much sun can burn unprotected skin and cause permanent discoloration and damage to the dermis (the second layer of skin). (4) Most important, long-term exposure of unprotected skin can result in skin cancer.

Questions

Read the following questions. Circle the letter of the answer you think is correct.

1. Which <u>two</u> organizational patterns does this paragraph use?
   a. chronology; cause and effect
   b. order of importance; cause and effect
   c. order of importance; comparison and contrast
   d. cause and effect; comparison and contrast

2. Which sentence expresses the main idea of this passage?
   a. Sentence (1)
   b. Sentence (2)
   c. Sentence (3)
   d. Sentence (4)

3. According to the passage, what is the most important reason to avoid too much sun?
   a. It can dry skin.
   b. It can speed up the aging process.
   c. It can burn skin.
   d. It can cause skin cancer.

4. Which of the following can result from dry skin?
  a. burns
  b. a rash
  c. reduced elasticity
  d. permanent discoloration

EXERCISE 2

Note: Exercise 2 is considerably longer than any other passage you've had so far—but it's about the length you'll expect to see on standardized tests. If the length seems a bit scary, don't worry. Just read the story carefully and actively as you would any other passage.

The Tryout

A lark—that's what Alexander's family called him because he sang all the time. Personally, Alexander believed he sounded more like a crow, but it didn't concern him. He simply liked singing. He sang in the shower, he sang while he did his homework, and he sang while he walked to school. He couldn't have cared less what he sounded like, until Kevin started talking about the tryouts for the City Boys' Choir.

"Yeah, I'm attending the tryouts this weekend," he heard Kevin bragging one day in class. "With my voice, I'm pretty much guaranteed a spot. I imagine they'll want me to perform lots of solos, too." Everyone around school knew that Kevin had a fantastic singing voice. Normally, Alexander just ignored him, but while he was walking home from school (singing as usual), he kept imagining himself as a member of the boys' choir. Wouldn't it be fun, he thought, to sing competitively with other kids and have someone actually teach him about singing?

Bright and early Saturday morning, Alexander's mom dropped him off at the auditorium where the tryouts were being held. Alexander took a deep breath, walked into the building, registered at a large table, and then joined the other boys who were all chattering nervously in the hallway. The only one who didn't look nervous was Kevin. And why should he be? Kevin had been taking lessons for years and had won numerous competitions. Alexander, on the other hand, had never taken a musical lesson in his life, much less had performed for an audience.

Fortunately, before Alexander had a chance to get too nervous, the choir director, Mr. Robeson, walked in and immediately got things started. He had each boy stand up on the auditorium stage, announce himself, and sing a song. When Alexander's turn came, he pretended he was singing in the shower and did his best to ignore the scribbling of the people sitting in the front row, who were diligently taking notes on his performance. He felt satisfied when he was done, at least until Kevin's turn came. As Kevin's confident voice filled the room, Alexander realized that he would never sound that good.

After the boys had finished their individual performances, Mr. Robeson put them into groups of four or five and asked them to sing again, this time as a group. Alexander thoroughly enjoyed singing with the other boys. He did his best to blend his voice with theirs. Kevin's group sang right after Alexander's, and even with four other boys singing, Kevin's voice was clear, distinct, and completely unmistakable; it seemed to reach the farthest corners of the auditorium.

When the groups finished singing, Mr. Robeson began the interview process. He asked Alexander about his performance experience, any music lessons he'd had, any training he'd received. All Alexander could say was, "I just really enjoy singing. I sing all the time, and I want to learn more." He kept imagining the lengthy and detailed answers Kevin would give to each of Mr. Robeson's questions.

Afterwards, Alexander slunk miserably out of the building and climbed into his mother's car.

The next afternoon Alexander anxiously pedaled his bicycle over to the auditorium where a list of new members was supposed to be posted. He didn't think his name would be on the list, but he was curious to see who'd made it. Quickly, he scanned the list, and then he read it again more deliberately. There must have been some mistake. His name was on the list, and Kevin's name was not.

Just then the door opened and Mr. Robeson strolled out. "Um, excuse me, Mr. Robeson," stammered Alexander. "What happened? How did I make the choir?"

"You love singing, and what better quality could a choir member have? Your voice isn't the best I've ever heard, but with training I think it will improve quite a bit. That improvement will take a lot of practice, however. You *are* willing to practice, aren't you?"

"Of course I am. But, what about Kevin? Why didn't he make it? He has such a good voice."

"Talent alone is not enough," said Mr. Robeson. "We need boys who are willing to work hard. Even the best singers in the world must continue to practice. Just think about it, Alexander. This is a choir where all of the members are equal. We weren't looking for soloists. We were looking for boys who seemed to have the right voice and attitude to be part of a choir. Enough about tryouts, though. Will we see you at choir practice this week?"

"Absolutely, Mr. Robeson!" Alexander said. He climbed back onto his bicycle and rode home, singing the whole way.

Questions

Read the following questions. Circle the letter of the answer you think is correct.

5. What is the overall organizing principle of this passage?
   a. chronology
   b. order of importance
   c. comparison and contrast
   d. cause and effect

6. Which organizational pattern is used *within* the third paragraph?
   a. chronological
   b. order of importance
   c. comparison and contrast
   d. cause and effect

7. Why did Alexander try out for the choir?
   a. because he has a terrific voice
   b. because he loves to sing
   c. because he practiced hard
   d. because he was good friends with Kevin

8. According to this story, in what way are Kevin and Alexander *alike*?
   a. They both love to sing.
   b. They both have great voices.
   c. They both made the choir.
   d. They both tried out for the choir.

9. Which is the correct order of events that took place during the tryout?
   a. singing in a group, singing alone, interviewing with Mr. Robeson
   b. singing in a group, interviewing with Mr. Robeson, singing alone
   c. singing alone, singing in a group, interviewing with Mr. Robeson
   d. interviewing with Mr. Robeson, singing alone, singing in a group

10. Reread the following sentence from the story.

When Alexander's turn came, he pretended he was singing in the shower and did his best to ignore the scribbling of the people sitting in the front row, who were diligently taking notes on his performance.

The word *diligently* in this sentence probably means
   a. carefully and attentively.
   b. slowly.
   c. loudly and rudely.
   d. sloppily.

11. According to the story, in what way is Alexander *different* from Kevin?
   a. Alexander has more singing experience.
   b. Alexander has no musical training.
   c. Alexander has won fewer competitions.
   d. Alexander has a better voice.

12. When Alexander sang by himself in the audition, he
   a. pretended he was singing in a concert.
   b. pretended he was singing to Kevin.
   c. pretended he was singing in the shower.
   d. pretended he was conducting the choir.

13. According to Mr. Robeson, what characteristic does Alexander have that Kevin does not?
   a. Alexander has the right attitude.
   b. Alexander has a better schedule for coming to practice.
   c. Alexander was brave enough to try out.
   d. Alexander didn't want to be a soloist.

14. In which of the following sentences is Mr. Robeson expressing an *opinion*?
   a. "Will we see you at choir practice next week?"
   b. "We weren't looking for soloists."
   c. "Your voice isn't the best I've ever heard, but with training I think it will improve quite a bit."
   d. "You love singing."

15. Which of the following events occurred *immediately after* Alexander sang with a group?
   a. Alexander interviewed with Mr. Robeson.
   b. Alexander listened to Kevin's group sing.
   c. Alexander joined Kevin's group to sing again.
   d. Alexander sang alone.

Skill Building until Next Time

1. Look again at the passages you read in Lessons 1–5. What organizational structures do you notice at work in those paragraphs?

2. As you read (and write) in the next few days, be aware of the structure of each paragraph and of passages as a whole. Choose one of the passages you like a lot, and try to identify the author's overall organizational strategy as well as other strategies he or she may use throughout the text.

ANSWERS

EXERCISE 1
Section 2 Practice

1. **b.** This paragraph lists three effects of too much sun and lists them from least to most important.

2. **a.** The first sentence is a topic sentence that clearly expresses the main idea of the paragraph.

3. **d.** The beginning of the fourth sentence tells us that this is the most important effect.

4. **c.** The second sentence explains that dry skin can have two results (effects): It can reduce its elasticity and speed up the aging process.

EXERCISE 2

5. **a.** This is a story organized chronologically, from Alexander's interest in trying out for the choir to the results of his tryout. The story also uses comparison and contrast and cause and effect, but chronology is the only organizing principle that works throughout the entire story.

6. **c.** At the end of the third paragraph, the author directly contrasts Alexander's singing experience to Kevin's.

7. **b.** The first paragraph stresses just how much Alexander likes to sing, and the second paragraph tells us he thought it would "be fun" to sing competitively and learn more about singing. This is also the best answer because none of the other possible answers are true: He did not have a terrific voice, he did not practice hard (he only sang for fun), and he was not good friends with Kevin.

8. **d.** The only similarity clear in the story is that they both tried out for the choir. We can guess that Kevin loves to sing, but that is never mentioned in the story, and the fact that he does not have the right attitude suggests that maybe he *doesn't* like to sing all that much. We know that Alexander does not have a great voice, so (b) is incorrect, and we also know that Kevin did not make the choir, so (c) can't be the correct answer.

9. **c.** When Mr. Robeson gets things started, he first "had each boy stand up . . . and sing a song." Then, "after the boys had finished their individual performances, Mr. Robeson put them into groups." Finally, "When the groups finished singing, Mr. Robeson began the interview process." Notice the carry over clues in both the second and third steps.

10. **a.** *Diligently* means *carefully, attentively.* Given the context of the sentence, this is the meaning that makes the most sense. There seem to be a lot of boys competing for the choir, and there are three separate steps in the tryout, so the process seems to be taken very seriously.

11. **b.** Unlike Kevin, Alexander has no musical training. This is stated in the third paragraph: "Alexander . . . had never taken a musical lesson in his life."

12. **c.** This specific fact is stated in the fourth paragraph: "When Alexander's turn came, he pretended he was singing in the shower."

13. **a.** Mr. Robeson's answer is all about attitude. He likes it that Alexander loves to sing and that Alexander seems willing to work hard and practice. He tells Alexander, "We were looking for boys who seemed to have the right voice *and attitude* to be part of a choir."

14. **c.** The first choice is a question, so it is neither a fact nor an opinion. Both (b) and (d) state facts: Robeson and the others "weren't looking for soloists"—they wanted boys who wanted "to be part of a choir"—and of course the fact that

Alexander loves to sing is repeated throughout the story. In addition, the phrase "I think" is a good clue that (c) offers an opinion.

15. b. In the fifth paragraph, after Alexander sings with his group, we read: "Kevin's group sang right after Alexander's," and Alexander could clearly hear Kevin's voice. Thus, (b) is the correct answer.

If You Missed:	Then Study:
Question 1	Lesson 7, 9
Question 2	Lesson 2
Question 3	Lesson 4, 7
Question 4	Lesson 4
Question 5	Lesson 6
Question 6	Lesson 8
Question 7	Lesson 4, 9
Question 8	Lesson 8
Question 9	Lesson 6
Question 10	Lesson 3
Question 11	Lesson 8
Question 12	Lesson 4
Question 13	Lesson 8
Question 14	Lesson 4
Question 15	Lesson 6

S·E·C·T·I·O·N

LANGUAGE AND STYLE

3

In most of the passages you've read so far, the author's ideas and purpose have been very clear. But what happens when they're not? What if the writer doesn't provide a topic sentence that clearly expresses the main idea? What about stories and poems? How do you figure out what the author is trying to say?

The good news is that no matter what the text, if you read carefully, you'll find plenty of clues about its meaning. Some of the most helpful clues are found in the writer's *language* and *style*. How does the author write? What types of words does the author use? What types of sentences? What point of view does he or she choose?

The lessons in this section are all about language and style. You'll learn about:

- point of view
- word choice
- style
- tone

You'll see how authors use these elements to create meaning. Then you'll put it all together in Lesson 15.

L · E · S · S · O · N

POINT OF VIEW

11

LESSON SUMMARY

This lesson is about **point of view:** the perspective that writers use to tell a story. You'll learn the three main points of view and the effects each point of view has on the reader.

Imagine that you're at a magic show. On stage, the magician is sawing his assistant in half. From the tenth row, it looks like he really has cut her in two! But she's alive and smiling. Magic!

Now imagine that you're still at the magic show, but this time you're not in the audience—you're backstage. From where you are, what do you see now? The trick looks quite different. From this point of view, you can see the assistant open a trap door for her legs. You can see the magician place a curtain over part of her body. You can see, in fact, how the "magic" works—and it's no magic at all.

In both cases, the magician and his assistant did the same thing. But what you saw was very different, because what you saw depended upon your point of view.

Point of view (also often called *perspective*) is the person or position through which you see things. You can look at an object, for example, from many different points of view. You can look at it from above, below, behind, beside, and so on. How you see the object and what you see often depends upon your position as you're looking at it.

You can look at ideas and events from many different points of view, too. At the magic show, there were two different points of view: that of someone in the audience and that of someone backstage. Both people saw the same event, but they saw two very different things. This is true of most things in life, and that's why it's so important to be aware of point of view.

In writing, the point of view is like a filter. It's the **voice** through which the writer shares his or her ideas. What readers hear depends upon who is telling it to them. Thus, point of view is an important decision for writers to make. Who will talk to the reader? Who will **narrate** the story? (In stories, the person who tells the story is called the narrator.)

THE THREE POINTS OF VIEW

There are three points of view writers can use: the **first-person, second-person,** and **third-person** point of view. Each point of view is available to writers, but only one of them will create the exact effect that the writer desires. That's because each point of view works differently and creates a different relationship between reader and writer.

THE FIRST-PERSON POINT OF VIEW

The first-person point of view is a very personal point of view. The writer uses the pronouns *I, me, my, we,* and *us.* Thus, the writer or narrator using the first-person point of view shares his or her own feelings, experiences and ideas with the readers. Here are two examples:

I couldn't wait for the weekend. I would finally get to meet my relatives from Romania, the people I'd been writing to for years but had never seen.

We wandered around for hours and finally admitted that we were hopelessly lost. What were we going to do now?

THE SECOND-PERSON POINT OF VIEW

The second-person point of view uses the pronoun *you.* By doing so, the writer or narrator puts the reader in his or her shoes or in the situation he or she is describing. Here are the examples above rewritten in the second-person point of view:

You couldn't wait for the weekend. You would finally get to meet your relatives from Romania, the people you'd been writing to for years but had never seen.

You wandered around for hours and finally admitted that you were hopelessly lost. What were you going to do now?

THE THIRD-PERSON POINT OF VIEW

The third-person point of view offers readers the voice of an "outsider." There is usually no direct reference to the writer or narrator (the first person *I* or *we*). Instead, the writer uses the pronouns *he, she, it,* or *they.* Here are our examples again, rewritten in the third-person point of view:

She couldn't wait for the weekend. She would finally get to meet her relatives from Romania, the people she'd been writing to for years but had never seen.

They wandered around for hours and finally admitted that they were hopelessly lost. What were they going to do now?

DETERMINING POINT OF VIEW

Of course, writers can't be restricted to one pronoun, so sometimes you need to read carefully to determine which point of view the writer is using. For example, read the following sentence:

> I was watching her carefully, wondering what she would say to you.

Here, we seem to have all three points of view, don't we? There's the first-person *I*, the second-person *you*, and the third-person *her* and *she*. But really this sentence only uses *one* point of view. The question to ask is, *who* is talking? Who is telling the story or sharing the information? The answer should tell you the correct point of view. In this case, it is clearly a first-person point of view.

EXERCISE 1

Determine the point of view in the following sentences by circling the letter of the correct answer.

1. As Xavier held tightly to the rope, Paul used all of his strength to pull his friend up out of the gorge.
   a. first-person
   b. second-person
   c. third-person

2. By now you're settled into your routine. You wake up at 5:00 A.M., walk the dogs, shower, gulp down a quick breakfast, and meet Mr. Walton in the cafeteria for a challenging game of chess before school.
   a. first-person
   b. second-person
   c. third-person

3. I thought and thought but could not come up with any reason why she would be angry with me.
   a. first-person
   b. second-person
   c. third-person

4. We'd never talked much before, and he always thought I was a shy person, so he couldn't believe how much I talked when we went out to dinner.
   a. first-person
   b. second-person
   c. third-person

5. They knew that he wanted to join their club, but they were afraid to make an exception for him.
   a. first-person
   b. second-person
   c. third-person

THE EFFECT POINT OF VIEW

As we've already stated, point of view is important because each point of view creates a different effect.

THE RELATIONSHIP TO THE READER

Perhaps the most important difference among the points of view is the kind of relationship they create between reader and writer. Read the two paragraphs below to see for yourself. The first paragraph is from "The Tryout," which you read in Lesson 10 and which is told in the third-person.

> The next afternoon, Alexander anxiously pedaled his bicycle over to the auditorium where a list of new members was supposed to be posted. He didn't think his name would be on the list,

but he was curious to see who'd made it. Quickly, he scanned the list, and then he read it again more carefully. There must have been some mistake. His name was on the list, and Kevin's name was not.

This paragraph is the same passage rewritten in the first-person point of view.

The next afternoon, I anxiously pedaled my bicycle over to the auditorium where a list of new members was supposed to be posted. I didn't think my name would be on the list, but I was curious to see who'd made it. Quickly, I scanned the list, then I had to read it again more carefully. There must have been some mistake. My name was on the list, and Kevin's name was not.

Though these paragraphs tell the same story, the effects are quite different. When the story is told from the first-person point of view, there's suddenly a *direct contact* between the reader and the storyteller. Here, Alexander himself is speaking directly to us. When the story is told in the third-person, *someone else*, an outside narrator, is telling Alexander's story to us. There's no direct contact.

The first-person point of view, then, tends to create a sense of *closeness* between reader and writer (or narrator). The writer (or narrator) shares his or her feelings and ideas with us. The relationship between reader and writer is personal, often informal, friendly, and open.

The third-person point of view, on the other hand, creates more *distance* between reader and writer (or narrator). With the third-person point of view there's no direct person-to-person contact. Instead, someone else (often an unnamed narrator) is speaking to the reader. The relationship between the reader and the writer (or narrator) is therefore more formal, less friendly, and less open.

EXERCISE 2
Questions

Make the following sentences less formal and more personal by switching the point of view.

1. The ad makes readers feel good about themselves.

   _____

   _____

   _____

2. The students are upset about the change in the lunch menu._____

   _____

   _____

3. People often feel betrayed when someone breaks a promise._____

   _____

   _____

SUBJECTIVITY VERSUS OBJECTIVITY

Another important difference between the points of view is the level of **subjectivity** or **objectivity** they create. Sometimes, it's important *not* to be too friendly and informal. The first-person point of view may make the reader feel close to the writer, but the first-person point of view is a *personal* point of view. It is therefore **subjective**. Ideas often carry more weight if they are presented in an **objective** way. An objective person is outside the action; he or she is not personally involved. Therefore, his or her ideas are more likely to be fair to everyone. But someone involved in the action is subjective and therefore affected by the situation. His or her ideas may be based on personal feelings and desires and may be limited by what he or she was able to see.

Subjective: based on the thoughts, feelings, and experiences of the speaker or writer (first-person point of view)

Objective: unaffected by the thoughts, feelings, and experiences of the speaker or writer (third-person point of view)

To see the difference, read the following sentences carefully.

> A: I think a school uniform policy would hurt us more than it would help us.

> B: A school uniform policy would hurt students more than it would help them.

Which sentence offers a subjective point of view? Which is more objective? Clearly, Sentence A is written from the first-person point of view—and not just any first person, but a student's point of view. Sentence B, on the other hand, may still have been written by a student, but it is written in an objective, third-person point of view.

If you were making an argument against a school uniform policy, the objective, third-person point of view would probably be more convincing. Why? Because it suggests that you are not directly involved in the action or situation and therefore don't have a personal stake in the issue. It suggests that you have a more objective (and therefore more reasonable) opinion on the issue because you are an outsider. A first-person point of view, on the other hand, suggests that you are directly involved and have something personal at stake.

Of course, writers often use the third-person point of view to state very subjective opinions. But with the third-person point of view, opinions *appear* more objective—and that makes a bigger difference than you might think. See Practice 3 for an example of this.

EXERCISE 3
Questions

The following sentences use the first-person point of view. Change the point of view to the third-person to make the statements seem more objective.

1. Teacher: I think we deserve an additional period each day for class preparation. _____

    _____

    _____

2. Student: We should get less homework. I often feel overwhelmed by how much schoolwork I have to do at home._____

    _____

    _____

3. Parent: I often wonder if I'm doing the right thing for my children._____

    _____

    _____

WHAT ABOUT THE SECOND-PERSON POINT OF VIEW?

Indeed, what *about* the second-person point of view? When do writers use this pronoun, and what are its effects?

REFERRING TO THE READER

When writers write, they must decide how to refer to themselves or to the narrator. They must also decide how to refer to the reader. They can address the reader in two ways: with the second person *you* or with the third person *he, she,* or *it*.

Writers use the second person *you* to address the reader directly. Here's an example. Imagine that on your first day of school, you get the following letter.

Welcome to South Mountain High! In addition to a nationally recognized teaching staff, South Mountain also offers you many extracurricular activities to enhance your learning experience. You might want to join the Drama Club, the Math Team, or the South Mountain Student Volunteer Association. Please read the attached description of student clubs and activities and let us, in Student Services, know if you have any questions. Club Day will be held on Thursday, September 19.

Now imagine that you got this letter instead.

Welcome to South Mountain High! In addition to a nationally recognized teaching staff, South Mountain also offers students many extracurricular activities to enhance the students' learning experiences. Students can join the Drama Club, the Math Team, or the South Mountain Student Volunteer Association. Please read the attached description of student clubs and activities. Any questions should be addressed to Student Services. Club Day will be held on Thursday, September 19.

Which letter would you rather receive? More likely, you'd rather receive the first letter. That's because the first letter speaks directly to you; the writer addresses the reader with the second-person pronoun. In this letter, you are an individual, not a category (students). The first letter also comes *from* a person—the folks in Student Services, who use the first person *us* to refer to themselves. The result is a friendly person-to-person communication.

In the second letter, on the other hand, the reader isn't addressed at all. The letter never names *you* as the new student. This isn't necessarily because the writers mean to be impersonal, though. It could be that the writers intended this letter for a much wider audience, including parents and teachers, not just students.

GETTING THE READER INVOLVED

Writers also use the second-person point of view for another reason: to make readers feel directly involved in the action. Imagine, for example, that the writer of "The Tryout" put *you* in Alexander's shoes.

The next afternoon, you pedal anxiously over to the auditorium where a list of new members is supposed to be posted. You don't think your name will be on the list, but you're curious to see who's made it. Quickly, you scan the list . . . and then you read it again more carefully. There must have been some mistake! Your name is on the list, and Kevin's name is not.

How do you feel after reading this passage? Could you imagine yourself in Alexander's shoes?

Writers also use the second-person point of view in arguments when they want readers to imagine themselves in certain situations. Take the school uniform policy situation once more as an example, and read the following passage.

Imagine what it would be like if every morning, when you woke up, you knew exactly what you were going to wear. In fact, you'd know exactly what *everyone* in school was going to wear, because you are all required to wear uniforms. As you walk down the hall, you wouldn't be able to recognize your friend by her favorite sweater. You wouldn't be able to wear the stylish *and* comfortable pants you got for your birthday. You'd look just like everyone else in your navy blue sweater, white oxford shirt, and navy blue skirt.

As an introduction to an argument against a school uniform policy, this would probably be pretty effective—and certainly more effective than the same paragraph in the third-person point of view.

EXERCISE 4
Questions

Read the sentences below and decide which point of view is best for each writing situation. Explain why you believe this point of view would be effective.

1. You are the president of the new South Mountain High School Volunteer Association and you are writing a description of the association for a school brochure. _____

   _____

   _____

2. You are writing an editorial for the school newspaper. Your purpose is to convince students to keep the school property clean. _____

   _____

   _____

3. You are writing a letter to your school's PTA. Your purpose is to thank the PTA for an award you received. _____

   _____

   _____

LESSON SUMMARY

In writing, the point of view is the "person" through which the writer tells the story or shares information. The first-person point of view uses the pronouns *I*, *me*, and *we*. It is a personal point of view because the writer or narrator is speaking directly to the reader; therefore, it is also the most subjective point of view. The second-person point of view uses the pronoun *you*, putting the reader in the writer's or narrator's shoes. The third-person point of view presents information from an outsider's perspective and uses the pronouns *he, she, it,* or *they.*

You can see by now how important point of view is in writing, for each point of view creates a different effect. Sometimes it brings the reader and writer closer together (the first-person point of view); sometimes it pushes them apart (the third-person point of view). Sometimes it makes an argument more convincing through third-person objectivity, because the speaker is not directly involved in the action. Sometimes an argument is more convincing through second-person involvement. Still other times the argument is more convincing in the first-person point of view because of the intimacy that perspective creates.

Skill Building until Next Time

1. Think about the last conflict you had with someone. Describe the conflict first from your point of view using the first-person pronoun *I*. Then, tell the story again from another person's point of view. Use the first-person pronoun *I* again. Finally, tell the story from an outsider's perspective using the third-person point of view. How does the story change when the point of view changes? Which accounts are subjective? Which account is most objective?

2. Take something that you read today and change its point of view. For example, say you read a short story told in the first-person. Change it to third-person. How does the new point of view change the story and how you feel about the characters?

ANSWERS

EXERCISE 1
1. c. third-person
2. b. second-person
3. a. first-person
4. a. first-person
5. c. third-person

EXERCISE 2
1. The ad makes me feel really good about myself.
2. We're very upset about the change in the lunch menu.
3. I often feel betrayed when someone breaks a promise.

EXERCISE 3
Answers may vary slightly, but some may look like this.
1. Teachers deserve an additional period each day for class preparation because they have many papers to grade.
2. Students should be assigned less homework. They often feel overwhelmed by how much schoolwork they have to do at home.
3. Parents often wonder if they're doing the right thing for their children.

EXERCISE 4
1. For this letter, the third-person point of view is probably best. Any description will probably be read by a large audience, including students, parents, teachers, and administrators, so it would be best if I aimed for an official and objective point of view.
2. For this letter, you might use the second-person point of view to help readers imagine themselves looking at the trash around campus and feeling good about cleaning it up.
3. For this letter, the first-person point of view is definitely best. I would want my letter to be warm and personal.

L·E·S·S·O·N WORD CHOICE

LESSON SUMMARY

This lesson focuses on **diction,** the words writers choose to express meaning. A small change in word choice can have a big impact. You'll learn how to watch for word choice clues that reveal meaning.

W hat made Sherlock Holmes such a good detective? Was he just that much smarter than everyone else? Did he have some sort of magical powers? Could he somehow see into the future or into the past? No. Sherlock Holmes was no fortune-teller or magician. So what was his secret?

His powers of **observation.**

In Lesson 1, you learned how to become an active reader. One of the things active readers do is *look for clues.* So far you've learned, among other things, to look for clues for determining the main idea, the structure, and the point of view. Now we're going to focus on the clues writers offer through diction: the specific words writers choose to describe people, places and things. A writer's word choice can reveal an awful lot about how the writer feels about his or her subject.

MAKING OBSERVATIONS AND DRAWING CONCLUSIONS

Writers make a lot of decisions. They decide what to say and how to say it. They choose whether to clearly state their ideas or *suggest* them. If they only suggest them, then they need to decide what clues to leave for their readers, and who must find and interpret those clues.

> By looking closely, you can see the writer's clues that will help you understand the text. Word choice clues can come in the following forms:
>
> - particular words and phrases that the author uses
> - the way those words and phrases are arranged in sentences
> - word or sentence patterns that are repeated
> - important details about people, places, and things

Detective work is a two-part process. First, a detective must find the clues. But the clues alone don't solve the case. The detective must also **draw conclusions** based on those clues. These conclusions are also called **inferences.** Inferences are conclusions based on reasons, facts, or evidence.

The same sort of process takes place in reading. You need to look for clues and then draw conclusions based on those clues. What is the writer trying to say? Good conclusions come from good observations.

To be a better reader, be more like Sherlock Holmes: be more observant. In "The Adventures of the Blanched Soldier," Sherlock Holmes tells a client: "*I see no more than you, but I have trained myself to notice what I see.*" You don't have to be a genius to be a good reader; you just have to train yourself to notice what you see.

OBSERVING WORD CHOICE

Here's a quick test of your observation skills. Read the two sentences below.

> **A:** A school uniform policy would reduce disciplinary problems.
>
> **B:** A school uniform policy would minimize disciplinary problems.

It's not hard to see the difference between these sentences. In Sentence A, the writer says the policy will *reduce* disciplinary problems; Sentence B, on the other hand, uses the word *minimize.* No big deal, right? After all, both sentences say that the uniform policy will result in fewer disciplinary problems. But there is a difference. One sentence is much stronger than the other because one *word* is actually much stronger than the other. *To minimize* is to reduce to the smallest possible amount. Thus, while both writers agree that a uniform dress code would lessen disciplinary problems, the writer of Sentence B feels that it would nearly eliminate them. The writer doesn't need to spell this out for you because his *word choice* should make his position clear.

Here's another example.

> **A:** The school board instituted a strict new dress code.
>
> **B:** The school board instituted a tyrannical new dress code.

Do these two sentences mean the same thing? Again, not quite. Both *strict* and *tyrannical* show that the dress code is tough, but they suggest very different levels of toughness. A *strict* dress code is not as tough as one that is *tyrannical.* Nor is it as troubling. After all, *tyrannical* means controlling others through force or threats. Thus, *strict* suggests that the policy is tough, but acceptable. *Tyrannical* suggests that the policy is tough and unacceptable.

DENOTATION AND CONNOTATION

Even words that seem to mean the same thing have subtly different meanings and sometimes not-so-subtle effects. For example, look at the words *slim* and *thin:* If you say your aunt is *thin,* that means one thing. If you say she is *slim,* that means something a little bit different. That's because *slim* has a different **connotation** from *thin.* Connotation is a word's *suggested* or implied meaning; it's what the word makes you think or feel. *Slim* and *thin* have almost the same **denotation**—their dictionary definition—but *slim* suggests more grace and class than *thin. Slim* is a very positive word. It suggests that your aunt is healthy and fit. *Thin,* however, does not. *Thin* suggests that your aunt is a little bit too skinny for her health. *Thin* and *slim,* then, have different connotations. So the word you choose to describe your aunt can tell others a lot. Mark Twain once said, *"The difference between the right word and the almost right word is like the difference between lightning and the lightning bug."*

EXERCISE 1
Questions
Below are several sentences with a blank. Under each sentence are three words or phrases that all have similar denotations, but different connotations. See how the sentence sounds with each word in the blank. Then rank those words by connotation, marking the word with the strongest connotation "1" and the word with the weakest, or most neutral, connotation "3."

Example: I'm feeling kind of _____ today.
_____down
_____depressed
_____discouraged

Ranked by connotation:
___3___ down
___1___ depressed
___2___ discouraged

1. Joe has been looking a little _____ lately.
_____unwell
_____sick
_____under the weather

2. Our new neighbors are _____.
_____well off
_____rich
_____loaded

3. It takes a lot of _____ to do what he did.
_____courage
_____guts
_____confidence

4. I'm totally _____.
_____worn out
_____beat
_____exhausted

5. She told him a _____.
_____lie
_____fib
_____half-truth

6. This is clearly a _____ situation.

_____risky

_____dangerous

_____life-threatening

READING BETWEEN THE LINES

Paying attention to word choice is particularly important when the main idea of a passage isn't clear. A writer's word choice doesn't just *affect* meaning; it *creates* it. For example, look at the following description from a teacher's evaluation for a student applying to a special foreign language summer camp. There's no topic sentence, but if you use your powers of observation, you should be able to tell how the writer feels about her subject.

As a student, Jane usually completes her work on time and checks it carefully. She speaks French well and is learning to speak with less of an American accent. She has often been a big help to other students who are just beginning to learn the language.

What message does this passage send about Jane? Is she the best French student the writer has ever had? Is she one of the worst? Is she average? To answer this question, you have to make an inference, and you must support your inference with specific observations. What makes you come to the conclusion that you do?

The diction of the paragraph reveals that this is a positive evaluation, but not a glowing recommendation. Here are some of the specific observations you might have made to support this conclusion:

- The writer uses the word *usually* in the first sentence. This means that Jane is good about meeting deadlines for work, but not great; she doesn't always hand in her work on time.

- The first sentence also says that Jane checks her work *carefully*. While Jane may sometimes hand in work late, at least she always makes sure it's quality work. She's not sloppy.

- The second sentence says Jane speaks French *well*. This is a positive word, but not a very strong one. Again, she's good, but not great. A stronger word like *fluently* or *masterfully* would make a big difference.

- The second sentence also tells us she's "learning to speak with less of an American accent." This suggests that she has a strong accent and needs to improve in this area. It also suggests, though, that she is already making progress.

- The third sentence tells us that she often helps "students who are just beginning to learn the language." From this we can conclude that Jane has indeed mastered the basics. Otherwise, how could she be a big help to students who are just starting to learn?

By looking at the passage carefully, then, you can see how the writer feels about her subject.

EXERCISE 2
Questions

Read the paired sentences below, making careful observations as you read. Then answer the inference questions that follow. Be sure that you can support your answers with specific observations from the sentences.

Pair 1

A. Let's get together as soon as possible.

B. Let's meet as soon as we are able.

1. Which sentence suggests that the writer has a *more formal* relationship with the reader?_____

_____

_____

2. Which sentence suggests that the writer is more anxious to meet with the reader?_____

_____

_____

Pair 2
A. Rhonda has a very colorful way of speaking.
B. Rhonda has a very showy way of speaking.

3. Which sentence is more critical of Rhonda? How can you tell?_____

_____

_____

Pair 3:
A. They have been meeting in the hope of clearing up their differences.
B. They have begun negotiations in an attempt to resolve their conflict.

4. Which sentence seems more hopeful about the outcome?_____

_____

_____

5. Which sentence describes a more serious situation?_____

_____

_____

6. Which sentence suggests a more informal relationship between the parties that are meeting?

_____

_____

LESSON SUMMARY

Sherlock Holmes' secret was his power of observation. You, too, can learn to notice what you see by looking carefully at what you read. Notice the specific words the writer has used. Remember that writers choose their words carefully. They know that each word has a specific effect, and they want just the right word to convey their ideas.

Skill Building until Next Time

1. Think about how you choose your words. Do you use different words for different people? Imagine you are describing an event to a family member and then to a classmate. Would you describe it the same way? Or would your word choice be different? Do you think carefully about what you say and which words you will use? How aware are you of your word choice? Write down both descriptions and compare them.

2. Take another look at something you read recently. This could be an ad or a full-length article. What words does it use to appeal to its audience. Why are they effective?

ANSWERS

EXERCISE 1
1. 2, 1, 3
2. 3, 2, 1
3. 2, 1, 3
4. 2, 3, 1
5. 1, 2, 3
6. 3, 2, 1

EXERCISE 2

1. Sentence B suggests a more formal relationship between reader and writer. In Sentence B, the writer uses the word *meet* while the writer of Sentence A uses the less formal *get together*.

2. Sentence A suggests that the writer is more anxious to meet with the reader. In Sentence A, the writer uses the phrase *as soon as possible*, while the writer of Sentence B uses the less urgent phrase *as soon as we are able*.

3. Sentence B is more critical. The word *showy* suggests that she's a bit *too* colorful.

4. Sentence A seems more hopeful, since it uses less serious words throughout: *meeting* instead of *negotiations; in the hope* instead of *in an attempt; clearing up* instead of the more serious *resolve;* and *differences,* which is much milder than *conflict.*

5. Sentence B clearly describes a more serious situation. See the answer for 4.

6. The word choice in Sentence A suggests a more informal relationship between the parties. They are *meeting,* not *negotiating;* they hope to *clear up* rather than *resolve;* they have *differences,* not a *conflict.* These words are not only less serious; they're also less formal.

L·E·S·S·O·N

STYLE

13

LESSON SUMMARY

Writers think carefully not only about the words they use but also about the kind of sentences they'll write. Will they be long or short? Full of description or right to the point? This lesson shows you how to analyze a writer's style and how style helps create meaning.

Y ou might think your best friend really knows how to dress with style. Or you might wish that you could update your wardrobe so that you could keep up with the latest style. But as far as you're concerned, style has to do with fashion, not writing, right? So what's it doing in a book about reading comprehension?

Actually, understanding style is very important to reading success. Writers use different structures to organize their ideas, and they also use different styles to express those ideas. Being aware of style helps you see what writers are up to.

Style is also important because it's often what makes us like or dislike certain writers or types of writing. For example, some people like stories with a lot of description and detail, while others like stories with lots of right-to-the-point action. You may not change your taste after this lesson, but you should be able to appreciate and understand all kinds of writers and styles.

Before we go any further, let's define **style**.

Style: a way of doing something—writing, speaking, dressing, and so on; the manner in which something is done.

In writing, style generally consists of three elements:

- sentence structure
- level of description and detail
- level of formality

SENTENCE STRUCTURE

Think about a table for a moment. How many different ways could you put a table together? It could have four legs, or just one in the middle. It could be round, rectangular, or square—or any other shape, for that matter. It could be thick or thin. It could be made of wood, plastic, or metal. It could seat two people or twenty. In other words, the possibilities and combinations are virtually endless.

The same goes for sentences. They can come in all kinds of shapes and sizes. They can be short and simple, or long and complex, with lots of ideas packed together. Writers can use mostly one kind of sentence, or they can use a range of sentence sizes and styles. Sometimes sentences will all sound the same; other times sentences will vary in word order, length, and structure.

Here's an example of two very different styles:

Paragraph A

A team works best when it is organized. The leader should have clear goals. The team members should have well-defined roles. Everyone should have specific deadlines.

Paragraph B

The key to an effective team is organization. The team leader must have clear goals, and it's the team leader's job to make sure the team members understand those goals. But how should you meet those goals? Deciding who does what is just as important. Team success depends upon everyone knowing exactly what is expected of him or her. Finally, all team members should have very specific deadlines for each job they are assigned.

Notice the following differences between these two paragraphs:

Paragraph A
- uses simple sentences
- uses the same sentence structure (type of sentence) throughout
- does not provide transitions between sentences
- has limited word choice, simple vocabulary

Paragraph B, on the other hand
- uses complex sentences
- has a lot of variety in sentence structure
- uses strong transitions between sentences
- has variety in word choice and a more sophisticated vocabulary

Which style do you prefer? Chances are that paragraph B sounds a lot better to your ear. Paragraph A is simple and clear, but it may sound dull because all the sentences follow the same simple pattern. They are all short, and there aren't any transitions. As a result, the paragraph sounds choppy.

Paragraph B, on the other hand, flows well. The sentences are longer and more varied. They sound more natural, because people speak in varied rhythms and in complex thoughts.

Here's another example of two passages with different sentence structures:

Paragraph A

Emma stared sadly out the window of the bus. Only 50 miles outside town was the farm. She thought about the farm all the time. She remembered the breathtaking view from her bedroom window. She remembered the creaky wooden floors of the old farmhouse. She especially remembered the animals.

Paragraph B

Emma stared sadly out the window of the bus. Only 50 miles outside town was the farm. She thought about the farm all the time, remembering the breathtaking view from her bedroom window, the creaky wooden floors of the old farmhouse, and especially the animals.

Again, we have two paragraphs that say the same thing but say it in very different styles. The second paragraph has only three sentences instead of six; it combines sentences three through six into one long sentence. But unlike the previous example, here the shorter sentences in paragraph A *don't* sound awkward or choppy. Instead, the repetition of "she remembered" creates a certain pleasing rhythm. This kind of *purposeful* repetition of a sentence pattern is called **parallelism.**

EXERCISE 1
Questions

Combine sentences and rewrite them in the paragraph below to create a new style.

Bicycles have always been popular forms of transportation. They are used for work and play. They are found on city streets and in small towns. They are even found in the mountains. The first mountain bikes were built in 1975. They were made to ride over rocky terrain. In order to handle the rocks and bumps on these trails, bicycles were built with heavy, balloon-like tires. They only had one speed. They also had coaster brakes.

_____

_____

_____

_____

_____

_____

_____

_____

_____

_____

LEVEL OF DESCRIPTION AND DETAIL

When we talk about the level of **description** and **detail,** we're looking at two things:

1. How **specific** is the author? Does he write "dog" (general) or "golden retriever" (specific)? Does she write "some" (general) or "three and a half pounds" (specific)?

2. How much **description** does the author provide? Does he write, "Mr. Gupta is my teacher" (nondescriptive) or "Mr. Gupta, my teacher, is a tall man with warm brown eyes and a curly mustache" (descriptive)?

Look carefully at the two sentences below as an example:

A. Jing-Mae just got a new bike.
B. Yesterday morning Jing-Mae went to Cycle World and bought an emerald green, 18-speed Diamondback mountain bike.

Both sentences tell you the same thing (that Jing-Mae bought a new bike), but the second version gives you a lot more information. The first writer keeps things general; he does not provide any description or detail. The second writer, though, gets specific and offers description and details.

Notice the increasing level of detail in the examples below. The first sentence is very general. The second sentence adds a little detail, and then the third gets even more specific.

1. My mom is a bank teller.
2. My mom is a bank teller at Pennview Savings.
3. My mom is a bank teller at Pennview Savings, the first bank in this city.

1. Let's meet after school on the corner.
2. Let's meet after school on the corner of Grove Street and Eighth Avenue.
3. Let's meet at 3:15 on the corner of Grove Street and Eighth Avenue.

The level of detail can reveal important information about the relationship between the reader and the writer. Sometimes, if a writer doesn't include a lot of detail, it's because the writer assumes the reader already knows certain information. For example, in the sentence "Let's meet after school on the corner," we can assume that the reader knows exactly which corner and what time to meet.

Description and detail are also important because they can help to draw out our emotions by helping us imagine a situation. For example, look at the following sentences:

A. When Paul heard the news, he jumped for joy.
B. When Paul heard the news, he jumped up and down on the couch, waving his arms wildly and screaming, "I did it! I did it!"

In Sentence B, we can *see* just how happy Paul was when he heard the news.

EXERCISE 2
Questions
Change the styles of the sentences below by adding specific description and detail.

1. He ate a huge breakfast this morning.
    Descriptive/detailed version: _____
    _____
    _____

2. The car sped down the street.
    Descriptive/detailed version: _____
    _____
    _____

3. The new computer lab has lots of equipment.
    Descriptive/detailed version: _____
    _____
    _____

FIGURATIVE LANGUAGE

An important aspect of style is **figurative language.** Figurative language includes **similes** and **metaphors.** A simile compares two things using the words *like* or *as.* A metaphor is stronger than a simile because it makes the comparison *without* the words *like* or *as.* Here's an example:

No figurative language	He is tall.
Simile	He is as tall as a skyscraper.
Metaphor	He is a skyscraper.

Figurative language is so effective because it helps readers picture what the writer is describing in an imaginative way. The writer could have said "He is seven feet, two inches tall," and that would have been very specific—one way to give us a clear picture of how tall he is. By using a simile or metaphor, though, the writer creates a different picture. It may be less *exact*, but it certainly is more *powerful*.

> **Note:** For similes and metaphors to work, the two things being compared must be sufficiently different. For example, it doesn't work to compare a moth to a butterfly. However, it *does* work to compare the way a butterfly's wings move and the way curtains flutter in the wind.

EXERCISE 3
Questions
Create similes and metaphors for the following sentences.

1. He has a violent temper.

   Simile: _____

   Metaphor: _____

2. She was running around crazily.

   Simile: _____

   Metaphor: _____

LEVEL OF FORMALITY

The third element of style is level of formality. Would you say to your principal, "Hey, dude, what's up?" Prob-

ably not. But you certainly might talk that way to your friends. You usually think about how formal or informal you should be before you talk to someone. The same goes for writing. Writers must decide how formal or informal they should be when they write. They make this decision based on their audience (whom they're writing for) and their purpose (why they're writing).

Writers can use slang, which is very informal; formal or ceremonious language; or something in between. They can address readers by their first names (casual) or by their titles (formal). For example, look at the different levels of formality in the sentences below:

A: Amelia, please come up here now.
B: Ms. Bravehart, please proceed to the front of the room immediately.

The first sentence is informal while the word choice in the second creates a much higher degree of formality. Here's another example:

A: I couldn't believe it. I mean, who would have guessed? I sure didn't! I had no clue, no clue at all. And I was the last person to find out, too. It figures.
B: I was deeply shocked; I had never suspected such a thing. Not surprisingly, I was the last person to become aware of the situation.

Notice the drastic difference in style. Though they both tell the same story and both use the personal, first-person *I*, there's clearly a different relationship to the reader. From the word choice and style—the short sentences, the very casual language—we can tell that the writer of passage A has a more informal, more friendly relationship with the reader than the writer of passage B. You feel the emotion of the writer in passage A much more strongly, too, because the language is more

LearningExpress Skill Builders • LESSON 13

informal, more natural. You get the idea that passage A is addressed to a friend while passage B might be addressed to an official.

EXERCISE 4

Questions

Rank the sentences below according to formality. Put a "1" next to the sentence that is most formal and a "3" next to the sentence that is most casual, and a "2" for a mid-range.

1. __ Your grades have improved.

   __ These calculations show that your class average has increased.

   __ Your grades are up!

2. __ You're doing great work, Sierra.

   __ Nice job, Sierra.

   __ Your performance is above our expectations, Sierra.

LESSON SUMMARY

Style is an important aspect of reading comprehension. Sentence structure, the level of description and detail, and the level of formality can reveal a lot about the writer's relationship to the reader. They also tell us about the writer's purpose and help us see and feel what the writer is describing.

Skill Building until Next Time

1. As you read, think about how things would sound if you changed the style. Make the sentences more formal or more casual. Add or cross out details and description. Change the sentence structure by combining sentences or breaking long sentences into shorter ones. How does the new style sound? What is the effect of the new style?

2. Look through things you've read recently to find examples of different writing styles. Consider why these authors have chosen different styles.

ANSWERS

EXERCISE 1

Answers will vary slightly. Here's one way to combine the sentences:

Bicycles have always been popular forms of transportation. Used for both work and play, they can be found on city streets, in small towns, and even in the mountains. Built in 1975, the first mountain bikes were made to ride over rocky terrain. In order to handle the rocks and bumps on these trails, bicycles were built with heavy, balloon-like tires. They had only one speed and coaster brakes.

EXERCISE 2

Answers will vary. Here's one possibility.

1. As usual, he ate a huge breakfast this morning: three eggs over-easy, a dozen banana pancakes, ten strips of bacon, a pear, two pieces of buttered rye toast, a glass of 2% milk, and a glass of orange juice.
2. The red convertible sped down Riverside Drive doing about 80 miles per hour.

3. The new computer lab on the fourth floor has ten PCs, ten blueberry colored IMacs, a color inkjet printer, and a scanner.

EXERCISE 3

Answers will vary. Here's one possibility:

1. **Simile:** He has a temper like a tornado.
   Metaphor: His temper is a tornado.

2. **Simile:** She was running around like the Mad Hatter.

Note: You might have been tempted to say "She was running around like a chicken with its head cut off." True, this is a simile, but it's also a **cliché**—an overused phrase. Try to avoid clichés in your writing. Instead, come up with a fresh image.
Metaphor: She was the Mad Hatter.

EXERCISE 4

1. 2, 1, 3
2. 2, 3, 1

L·E·S·S·O·N
TONE

14

LESSON SUMMARY

When you speak, your **tone** of voice actually conveys more meaning than your words. The same is true in writing. To understand what you read, you need to "hear" the writer's tone. This lesson shows you how.

Say this word out loud: "Sure."

How did you say it? Did you say it with a smile, as in, "Sure, any time"? Or did you stretch the word out, "*Suuuuure,*" as if you didn't believe what someone just said? Or did you ask it, as in, "Are you *sure* this is okay?"

How can there be so many ways to say *sure*? The word itself doesn't change; its denotation remains the same. So how can this one word express so many different things?

The difference, of course, comes from your **tone:** *how* you say the word. Your tone of voice expresses your attitude and therefore conveys what you really mean when you say "sure."

> **Tone:** the mood or attitude conveyed by words or speech.

When you listen to others, it's usually pretty easy to hear the tone of their voice. But how do you "hear" tone in writing? How can you tell how the words should sound? Say you come across the word "sure" as you're reading. How do you know whether to whisper it or shout it?

Think about how tone is created in speech. We create tone by how quickly or slowly we say a word, how loudly or softly we say it, and by our facial expressions and body language. When you read, though, you can't *hear* how the writer says something. And you certainly can't see the writer's facial expressions or body language. But you *can* use your powers of observation to determine tone. Three important clues will help you "hear" when you read:

- point of view
- word choice
- style

DETERMINING TONE

To better understand tone, let's compare writing to cooking for a moment. Think of words as ingredients. Those ingredients are put together to create a dish (an idea). Language and style are like the spices in a dish. Writers add them to give their sentences a certain flavor—that is, to create a specific tone.

To determine tone, then, you need to look carefully at the "ingredients." What has the writer put into the passage? What words has he or she chosen? What

kind of sentences? Which point of view? These elements of language and style are our clues.

Sometimes, the writer's clues make it easy. For example, look at the following sentence:

> "I really don't think I made the choir," said Alexander sadly.

Sadly tells us just how we should *hear* what Alexander said. Here's another example:

> "Ellen *always* gets her way! It's not fair!" Ginger shouted angrily.

Again, the key word *angrily* tells us just the tone to "hear" in our heads when we read this passage.

LOOKING FOR CLUES

Writers often provide this kind of clue when they're writing dialogue. But sometimes they don't; and many of the texts you'll read won't include any dialogue at all. So what clues do you look for then?

To answer that question, let's look at an example:

> "I just quit, that's all," Toby said, still looking down at the ground. "I just . . . quit."

How do we know *how* Toby says this? To determine tone, we need to look carefully at exactly what he says and what he is doing while he says it (the context).

First, notice that Toby repeats himself: He says, "I just quit" two times. The first time, he also says, "that's all"—a phrase that suggests he doesn't know what else to say or how to explain what happened. We can see that he's upset about the situation and doesn't want to talk about it. We can also infer that it was a difficult decision for Toby to make.

The second time Toby says, "I just quit," he includes a pause, which we can "read" from the . . . , called an ellipsis. Again, this pause suggests that he's uncertain of what to say or how to say it—that he doesn't want to talk about it. Punctuation can be an important clue in determining tone. An exclamation point, for example, tells you that someone is expressing a strong emotion. You'd then have to determine from the context whether that feeling is anger, joy, or some other emotion.

Another clue is that Toby is "still looking down at the ground." What Toby is doing suggests a couple of things: (1) that he's unhappy with his decision, (2) that he's embarrassed by it, and/or (3) that he knows he's disappointed the person he is speaking to (and therefore can't look that person in the eye).

With these three important observations and the inferences you can draw from them, you can take a pretty good guess at the tone. Does Toby say this loudly or softly? Probably quite softly. Most likely, Toby's words were said with a mixture of anger and sadness—more anger in the first part, more sadness in the second.

Now let's look at another example. Imagine Jennifer has just written a letter to the Lake Park Zoo suggesting that the zoo create Just the Facts signs for all of its exhibits. Below are two letters she might get in response. Read the two letters below carefully. They seem to say almost the same thing, but because they have two very different tones, their meaning is actually quite different.

Letter A
Dear Lake Park Zoo Visitor:

Thank you for your letter. We will take your suggestion into consideration. We appreciate your feedback.

Please visit us again soon.

Letter B
Dear Jennifer:

Thank you for your recent letter suggesting Just the Facts signs for each of our exhibits. We are taking your recommendation very seriously and truly appreciate your feedback.

We hope that you will visit us again soon.

If you looked carefully, you might have made the following observations:

- Letter A is addressed impersonally to a Lake Park Zoo Visitor. Letter B, on the other hand, is addressed personally to Jennifer.
- Both letters thank Jennifer for her letter, but only Letter B mentions specifically what Jennifer suggested in her letter.
- While Letter A tells Jennifer that someone at the zoo "will take [her] suggestion into consideration," Letter B tells her that someone is taking her recommendation "very seriously."
- The writer of Letter A says "We appreciate your feedback" while the writer of Letter B says that he "truly" appreciates her feedback.
- While Letter A concludes with "Please visit us again soon," Letter B offers a more personal invitation with "*We* hope that *you* will visit *us* again soon." This sentence also uses the word "*hope*."
- The sentences in Letter B are longer than those in Letter A, whose sentences are shorter and somewhat choppy.

Now, based on all of these observations (and the inferences you can draw from them), how would you describe the tone of Letter A?

a. sincere, honest
b. complimentary
c. indifferent, uncaring

Choice (c), indifferent, best describes the tone of Letter A. Through its word choice and sentence structure, its lack of detail and personal pronouns, it suggests a lack of concern or care. There's no indication that the writers of Letter A have actually read Jennifer's letter, so there's no indication that they plan to take her suggestion seriously. They are indifferent to it. Also, the sentence structure indicates that the writers have not put much thought into writing this letter. As a result, the sentences sound abrupt and even unappreciative.

Now, which word best describes the tone of Letter B?
a. cheerful
b. sincere
c. apologetic

In contrast to Letter A, the tone of Letter B is (b), sincere. The writer of the letter knows exactly what Jennifer suggested. (See how important specific details can be?) The writer has also taken the time to personalize the letter, and he or she has also chosen words that show the writer values Jennifer's feedback.

VARIETIES OF TONE

There are endless varieties of tones when we speak. Likewise, there are endless varieties of tone in writing. Here's a list of some of the more common words used to describe tone:

angry	indifferent
annoyed	insincere

anxious	ironic
apologetic	joyful
bold	matter-of-fact
bossy	mischievous
cheerful	mocking
complimentary	playful
confident	proud
critical	respectful
defeated	rude
demanding	sad
disrespectful	sarcastic
foreboding	secure
gloomy	sincere
grateful	somber
hesitant	threatening
humorous	timid
hopeful	uncertain
insecure	uplifting

Some of these words may be unfamiliar to you. If so, please look them up in a dictionary now and write their definitions in the margin and/or on your vocabulary list. These words will come in very handy when you read. They'll help you better understand meaning and help you identify tone. (Besides, you may need them for the practice exercise below!)

EXERCISE 1
Questions
Read the sentences below carefully to determine their tone. Read them out loud and listen to how they sound when you read them. With what kind of voice do you read? What's your tone? Use your instincts and power of observation when you circle the letter of the correct answer.

1. Um, I was wondering if maybe I could borrow your pen, if you don't mind. That is, if it isn't too much trouble.
   a. playful
   b. hesitant
   c. cheerful
   d. angry

2. Give me that pen!
   a. gloomy
   b. disrespectful
   c. demanding
   d. sad

3. For Pete's sake, get your own pen!
   a. absent-minded
   b. bold
   c. annoyed
   d. shy

4. May I borrow your pen, please?
   a. respectful
   b. timid
   c. anxious
   d. thoughtful

5. Remember, you need to be home by ten o'clock.
   a. bossy
   b. matter-of-fact
   c. ironic
   d. inspiring

6. You'd better be home by ten o'clock, or else!
   a. threatening
   b. sad
   c. demanding
   d. inspiring

7. Shi had stayed up all night working on his research paper. Finally, by 6:00 A.M., he had everything ready: cover page, essay, Works Cited page, and illustrations. This was the best essay he'd ever written, and he couldn't wait to present it to the class. He smiled as he showered and got ready for school.

   He smiled to everyone he passed on his way to the bus stop and smiled at the bus driver. He sat down in his usual seat and hummed to himself for a little while. Then he opened his bag. He wanted to admire his paper once more before his presentation. Of course, he'd left his paper on the kitchen table.
   a. proud
   b. ironic
   c. sad
   d. cheerful

8. "During the whole of a dull, dark, and soundless day in the autumn of the year, when the clouds hung oppressively low in the heavens, I had been passing alone, on horseback, through a singularly dreary tract of country . . . "—from Edgar Allan Poe, "The Fall of the House of Usher."
   a. gloomy
   b. mocking
   c. nostalgic
   d. hopeful

EXERCISE 2
Questions
To strengthen your understanding of tone, try this exercise. Change the tone of the passages below so that they convey a new mood. You can change words, add words, or delete words if necessary. Change the sentence structure if you like, too.

Example:

Change from: *matter-of-fact tone*
The tickets are sold out.

To: *disappointed tone*
Man, I can't believe the tickets are already sold out.
What a bummer!

1.   Change from: *apologetic tone*
I'm really, really sorry I got you in trouble.

   To: *indifferent tone*

   _____

   _____

2.   Change from: *annoyed tone*
Now what do you want?

   To: *respectful tone*

   _____

   _____

3.   Change from: *fearful tone*
Oh no—he's here!

   To: *joyful tone*

   _____

   _____

LESSON SUMMARY

Tone is the mood or attitude conveyed in speech or writing. Writers often rely on tone to get their messages across, so the ability to "hear" tone is essential for reading success. Look carefully for clues in the writer's language and style. Read sentences out loud and consider context to hear how writers want their words to sound.

Skill Building until Next Time

1.   Listen carefully to people today. How much of their message is conveyed by tone? Notice also how you use tone to convey meaning.

2.   Determine the tone of what you read today. How does the writer want his or her words to sound? What mood is he or she trying to convey? Even newspaper articles carry a certain tone. They often aim to be objective, but many articles are far from matter-of-fact in tone. This is especially true of reports on natural disasters or victims of violent crime.

ANSWERS

EXERCISE 1

1. **b.** The tone here is very hesitant. The writer is afraid to ask for what she wants and uses hesitant words and phrases. These include "um," "wondering," "if," "maybe," "if you don't mind," and "if it isn't too much trouble."

2. **c.** The writer is giving a strong command here. There is no hesitation in tone and no question being asked. Instead, the writer is ordering that something be done.

3. **c.** Here, the writer is annoyed. The phrase "for Pete's sake" expresses her frustration, and the exclamation point suggests that she's extremely annoyed.

4. **a.** This writer asks for a pen respectfully. First, she asks a clear and direct question. There's no pressure and no hesitation. Second, she uses the word "please."

5. **b.** This is a matter-of-fact statement. There's no suggestion of emotion; it's just a flat reminder. While it expresses a restriction, it doesn't come off bossy or demanding.

6. **a.** Here, the reminder has turned into a warning. The threat is conveyed in the phrases "you'd better" and "or else!" (Notice the exclamation mark).

7. **b.** *Irony* is created when what happens is the opposite of what was supposed to happen. Here, Shi had stayed up all night preparing his paper and presentation. He had everything ready, and he was excited about presenting his work. But his satisfaction and excitement turns into disappointment because he'd left his work at home. The irony is heightened by the way he smiles happily and confidently until he discovers his error.

8. **a.** Edgar Allen Poe is a master at creating tone in his stories. Here, "dull, dark and soundless," "oppressively," and "dreary" set a gloomy tone. This isn't going to be a happy romance but a horror story. Because of the number of gloomy words, you can even pick up the tone if you don't know what several of these words mean.

EXERCISE 2

Answers will vary. Here are some possibilities:

1. Too bad you got in trouble.
2. How can I help you?
3. At last! He's here!

L · E · S · S · O · N

PUTTING IT ALL TOGETHER

15

SECTION SUMMARY

This lesson reviews Lessons 11–14 and pulls together what you've learned in this section. You'll use point of view, word choice, style, and tone to understand what you read.

You've learned a lot about how writers use language to create meaning. Now you can add this to what you already know about how to be a good reader. But first, let's review the last four lessons.

WHAT YOU'VE LEARNED

Here's a quick review of each lesson about language and style:

Lesson 11: Point of View. You learned that writers choose a specific **point of view** to express their ideas. They can use the first person (*I, we*), second person (*you*), or third person (*he, she, it*) point of view. The first-person point of view creates closeness between the reader and writer and is a very subjective point of view. It directly expresses the feelings and ideas of the writer or narrator. The second-person point of view puts readers into the action and makes them feel involved. The third-person point of view is the most objective because the writer or narrator is not involved in the action. This point of view creates distance between the reader and writer.

Lesson 12: Word Choice. You learned to look carefully at the words writers use. Each word has a specific **connotation,** so different words will have a different impact even if their **denotation** is nearly the same. You learned to look closely at **diction** and draw conclusions based upon your observations.

Lesson 13: Style. You learned that **style** consists of three main elements: sentence structure, level of description and detail, and level of formality. Looking carefully at style can help you draw conclusions about the relationship between the writer and reader. Style can also reveal the writer's purpose and help you see and feel what the writer is describing.

Lesson 14: Tone. You learned that **tone** is the mood or attitude conveyed by the text. Tone is created by word choice and style and can dramatically affect meaning. You learned how to look for clues so you can determine how the words on the page should sound.

In Section 1, you learned how to be an active reader, how to find the main idea, how to define words from context, and how to distinguish between fact and opinion. In Section 2, you learned about four main writing structures: chronological order, order of importance, comparison and contrast, and cause and effect.

If any of these terms or strategies are unfamiliar, STOP. Take some time to review the term or strategy that is unclear.

SECTION 3 PRACTICE

In these practice exercises, you'll combine your knowledge of word power with everything else you've learned so far in this book. Read each passage actively and carefully. Then answer the questions that follow.

Note: If you come across unfamiliar words as you read these passages, do not look them up until *after* you've answered the questions below.

EXERCISE 1

The passage below is an advertisement for Mercury Shoes.

Help your feet take flight! Mercury Shoes promises you high quality and can save you from the aches and pains that runners often suffer.

Running magazine has awarded Mercury Shoes its "High Quality" rating for our breakthrough in shoe technology! By studying the feet of track-and-field champions and ultra-marathoners, we have developed a revolutionary sole construction that offers complete support for dedicated runners. Our unique combination of gel and air cushioning provides greater stability and incredible comfort.

Three types of Mercury Shoes are now available:

Cheetahs: A racing shoe that combines light weight with real support.

Mountain Goats: A superior trail-running shoe with great traction and stability even on muddy or slick trails.

Gray Wolves: A shoe that gives maximum support in order to minimize common injuries caused by mile after mile of training runs on hard pavement.

Questions

Read the following questions. Circle the letter of the answer you think is correct.

1. The ad uses which point of view to refer to its readers?
   a. first-person
   b. second-person
   c. third-person
   d. none of the above

2. The shoe names "Cheetahs," "Mountain Goats," and "Gray Wolves" reflect
   a. the personality of the shoe designer.
   b. the personality of the runner.
   c. the kind of running the shoe is designed for.
   d. the company's mascots.

3. Which of the following best describes the style of this passage?
   a. long sentences, lots of descriptive words
   b. lots of short, choppy, "bossy" sentences
   c. lots of similes and metaphors to create images
   d. slangy, informal words

4. Which of the following is presented as a *fact* in the ad?
   a. Mercury Shoes can save you from the aches and pains that runners often suffer.
   b. *Running* magazine has awarded Mercury Shoes its High Quality rating.
   c. Mercury Shoes has developed a revolutionary sole construction.
   d. Mountain Goats are superior trail-running shoes.

5. The shoe name Cheetahs suggests that
   a. the shoes will make you run faster.
   b. the shoes are designed to look like cheetah skins.
   c. the shoes provide extra support.
   d. the shoes are for those who like to run wild.

6. The tone of this passage is best described as
   a. pushy.
   b. matter-of-fact.
   c. hopeful.
   d. excited.

EXERCISE 2

You might recognize the first paragraph in the short story below.

A Day at the Nature Center

Emma stared sadly out the window of the bus. Only 50 miles outside town was the farm. She thought about the farm all the time, remembering the breathtaking view from her bedroom window, the creaky wooden floors of the old farmhouse, and especially the animals.

When Emma's parents sold their hundred-acre farm and moved to the nearby town of Carville, Emma had been enthusiastic. But when she got to the new school, she felt overwhelmingly shy around so many strangers.

With a sigh, Emma turned her attention back to the present. The bus came to a stop, and Emma climbed off with the rest of her Earth Studies classmates. "Welcome to the Leinweber Nature Center," her teacher, Mrs. Bowes, announced. "In a few minutes, a guide will give us a presentation about the area's native animals and habitat. After the presentation, you'll have a worksheet to complete while you explore the rest of the center. Now, I want everyone to find a partner."

Emma looked around apprehensively as her classmates began to pair up. She didn't have any friends yet—who would be her partner? Emma hesitated for a moment and then approached Julia, a talkative and outgoing girl who sat near her in class. "Could I be your partner?" Emma asked tentatively.

"Sure," said Julia warmly. "Let's go get the worksheet from Mrs. Bowes."

Together, the girls walked into the Leinweber Nature Center. They listened to the guide talk about how the workers at the center cared for injured and orphaned animals and how the center tried to recreate the animals' natural habitats as much as possible. Emma listened intently. She thought it would be wonderful to have a job that involved nurturing and caring for animals all day.

After the presentation, the girls examined their worksheets. "Let's see," said Julia "One of the things we're supposed to do is locate the rodent area and assist with feeding the baby squirrels. How big is a baby squirrel? Do you think we actually have to hold one? Maybe you should let me feed it while you watch." Julia was so excited that she fired off one question after another and didn't wait for a response from Emma.

Emma and Julia walked into the rodent area and stood there, looking around at all the rats, mice, chipmunks, and squirrels. "Hi there!" boomed an enthusiastic voice from behind them. "I'm Josh Headly, the keeper in charge of rodents. Did you come to see the squirrels?"

"Yes," said Emma, turning around with an eager smile on her face. "Do we actually get to feed the babies?"

"You sure do. Here—let me demonstrate the feeding procedure for you."

Josh showed them how to wrap a baby squirrel in a towel and hold the bottle of warm milk. Emma settled back into a chair, enjoying the warmth of the tiny ball of fur nestled in her hand. She flashed a smile over at Julia, but Julia, who was suddenly silent, was focusing on her own baby squirrel.

After the babies had finished eating, Josh asked, "Would you like to help feed the adult squirrels, too?"

Emma was quick to volunteer, but when Josh opened the first cage, the squirrel inside leaped out. Julia shrieked and tried to jump out of the way. Emma maintained her composure, bent down, held out her hand, and made quiet, soothing sounds. The runaway squirrel cocked its head to one side and seemed to listen to her. Quickly, while the squirrel was distracted by Emma, Josh reached over and scooped it up.

He smiled appreciatively. "Good job, Emma! It's not easy to remain calm when a wild animal gets out of its cage. I'm impressed!"

"Wow!" Julia chimed in. "You're always so quiet. I thought you were shy and scared of everything, but you're braver than I am if you can get close to a wild animal, even if it is just a squirrel."

"I'm only shy around people, not animals. And I used to live on a farm, so I know that when animals are scared or excited, you have to stay calm—even when you don't feel calm—if you want to help them."

Josh nodded in agreement. "You know," he began, "we've been taking applications for part-time volunteers to help out with the animals. Would you be interested in interviewing for a volunteer position here at the center?"

"Interested? I would love to work here! What an opportunity! Where are the application forms? When could I start?" Now it was Emma who was so excited she couldn't wait for a response.

That afternoon, in the bus on the way back to school, Emma sat next to Julia. A rush of new-found contentedness washed over her. Not only had she found a place full of animals to help take care of, but she had also made a new friend.

Questions

Read the following questions. Circle the letter of the answer you think is correct.

7. In which of the following ways are Emma and Julia **alike**?

  a. They both are very outgoing and talkative.

  b. They both feel comfortable around animals.

  c. They both have a class called Earth Studies.

  d. They both live on farms outside Carrville.

8. Which words best describe how Emma feels when her classmates first begin to pair up?

  a. angry and disappointed

  b. anxious and uncertain

  c. enthusiastic and joyful

  d. jealous and hurt

9. Reread the following sentence from the story:

Emma hesitated for a moment and then approached Julia, a talkative and outgoing girl who sat near her in class. "Could I be your partner?" Emma asked tentatively.

As it is used in the story, what does the word *tentatively* mean?

  a. carelessly

  b. eagerly

  c. forcefully

  d. cautiously

10. The author presents Julia as someone who:

  a. makes friends easily.

  b. is fun-loving but a poor student.

  c. knows a lot about animals.

  d. treats her friends badly.

11. Choose the correct sequence from the choices below.

  1 Julia and Emma sit together on the bus.

  2 A guide speaks about the nature center.

  3 Emma and Julia feed some baby squirrels.

  4 Josh introduces himself to the two girls.

  a. 3, 4, 2, 1

  b. 2, 4, 3, 1

  c. 1, 2, 4, 3

  d. 1, 4, 3, 2

12. This story is told from which point of view?

  a. first-person

  b. second-person

  c. third-person

  d. none of the above

13. Which word best describes Julia's tone in the following paragraph?

"Wow!" Julia chimed in. "You're always so quiet. I thought you were shy and scared of everything, but you're braver than I am if you can get close to a wild animal, even if it is just a squirrel."

  a. impressed

  b. jealous

  c. disbelieving

  d. embarrassed

14. Reread Emma's reaction to Josh's offer below.

"Interested? I would love to work here! What an opportunity! Where are the application forms? When could I start?"

The style of Emma's response
a. helps create an excited tone.
b. is repetitive and dull.
c. shows that she is unsure what to do.
d. reflects her shy nature.

15. Emma is happy at the end of the story because
a. she is no longer shy.
b. she will be paid well for her work at the nature center.
c. she has a new job and a new friend.
d. she thinks Josh has a crush on her.

Skill Building until Next Time

1. Review the "Skill Building" sections from Lessons 11–14. Try any "Skill Builders" you didn't do.

2. Write a few paragraphs about what you've learned so far. Begin each paragraph with a clear topic sentence. Here's an example: "Being observant will help me understand what I read." Then write several supporting sentences. Try to use at least one new word in your paragraphs.

ANSWERS

SECTION 3 PRACTICE

EXERCISE 1

1. b. In the first two sentences, the writers use the second person *you* to refer to readers. They use the first person *we* and *our* to refer to themselves in the second paragraph.

2. c. The shoes are named for the kind of running they're designed for. This is clear from each shoe's description. The Cheetahs (named after the fastest animal on earth) are "a racing shoe"; the Mountain Goats (named after these great climbers) are a "trail-running shoe." The Gray Wolves, meanwhile, are shoes designed for "training runs on hard pavement."

3. a. Most of the sentences are long and full of descriptive words such as "high quality," "revolutionary," "complete," "dedicated," "unique," "greater," and "incredible." Only two of the sentences are short, so this passage definitely does not have a "choppy" or "bossy" style (**b**). There are no similes or metaphors, though the first sentence is a form of **personification** that compares feet to a bird, so (**c**) is incorrect. Finally, there is no slang, so (**d**) is incorrect.

4. b. Answers (**a**), (**c**), and (**d**) offer *opinions* about the quality and benefits of the shoes. Answers (**c**) and (**d**) use clear, evaluative words—*revolutionary* and *superior*—to show they are stating an opinion. Answer **a** doesn't provide any evidence for this claim about the benefits of the shoes. Only (**b**) states a fact; this is the only statement here that is not debatable.

5. a. Cheetahs are the fastest four-footed animals on earth, reaching speeds of up to 60 miles per hour when they run. The name of the shoe, therefore, suggests that the shoe is built for speed and that if you wear them, you'll be able to run faster.

6. d. The two exclamation points and the number of positive, energetic words like "flight, breakthrough," and "revolutionary" create an excited tone. The description of the shoes is rather matter-of-fact (**b**), but overall, the passage expresses much more emotion. Most sentences express a high opinion about the quality of the shoes, and the exclamation points suggest strong enthusiasm.

EXERCISE 2

7. c. Julia "sat near [Emma] in class," and they pair up to complete an assignment for their Earth Studies teacher, Mrs. Bowes (paragraphs 3 and 4). Choice (**a**) is incorrect because we are told from the beginning (paragraph 2) that Emma is new to the school and "overwhelmingly shy." Later in the story, we know that the adult squirrel frightens Julia, so choice (**b**) is incorrect. And in paragraph 2, we learn that Emma *moved* from the farm, so neither girl lives on a farm outside Carrville (**d**).

8. b. Emma feels anxious and uncertain. The word choice in paragraph 4 provides the clues. Emma "looked around apprehensively." *Apprehensive* means feeling anxious or fearful. She also hesitates before she approaches Julia, which reflects her uncertainty. And she asks Julia *tentatively,* which means *hesitantly.* Even if you don't know what *apprehensively* and *tentatively* mean, you can assume that Emma would be anxious and uncertain because we are told she "felt overwhelmingly shy around so many strangers" when she arrives at her new school. Thus, she can't feel (**c**) enthusiastic and joyful. There's no evidence in the word choice or in Emma's personality that she'd feel (**a**) angry and disappointed or (**d**) jealous and hurt. These emotions would more likely come up if she'd been left out and couldn't find a partner.

9. d. Emma's shyness suggests that she wouldn't approach Julia forcefully (**c**) or eagerly (**b**). Another clue is that she hesitates before she asks. She also looks around "apprehensively," which suggests she will proceed cautiously, not carelessly (a).

10. a. Julia is described in paragraph 4 as "a talkative and outgoing girl," which suggests that she is someone who makes friends easily. She also responds to Emma "warmly." We know from her reaction to the adult squirrel that she does not know a lot about animals, so (c) is incorrect. She also treats Emma well, so (d) is incorrect. There is no evidence in the passage that Julia is a poor student, so (b) is also incorrect.

11. b. The story is told in chronological order. First, they listen to a guide (#2), then Josh introduces himself (#4) and shows them how to feed the squirrels (#3). The last event in the story is their ride home on the bus (#1).

12. c. All of the characters are referred to in the third-person point of view. They use the first-person *I* when they speak, but the narrator is *outside* the story and uses the characters' names and the pronouns *she* and *he* to refer to the characters.

13. a. Julia is very impressed with Emma's composure. A big clue to this tone is the word "Wow!" Julia also says that Emma must be "braver than I am," which again shows her respect for Emma.

14. a. Emma asks three questions and makes two statements, both with exclamation marks. All of her questions and statements are short and seem to tumble one on top of the other, as if Emma is too excited (like Julia earlier in the story) to wait for a response.

15. c. Emma has a new friend at the end of the story, but that doesn't mean she is no longer shy (a). Josh uses the word "volunteer" twice, so we know she won't be paid for her work (b). Finally, while it's clear that Josh respects Emma's composure and experience with animals, there's no evidence that he has a crush on her (d).

If You Missed:	Then Study:
Question 1	Lesson 11
Question 2	Lesson 4, 12
Question 3	Lesson 13
Question 4	Lesson 4
Question 5	Lesson 12
Question 6	Lesson 14
Question 7	Lesson 8
Question 8	Lesson 12
Question 9	Lesson 3
Question 10	Lesson 12
Question 11	Lesson 6
Question 12	Lesson 11
Question 13	Lesson 14
Question 14	Lesson 13
Question 15	Lesson 4

S · E · C · T · I · O · N 4

READING BETWEEN THE LINES

Now that you've studied how writers use structure and language, it's time to put your knowledge to work on more difficult texts. This week you'll look at passages that don't have a clear main idea. To understand this type of text, you need to look carefully for clues. You'll often need to "read between the lines" to see what the author means. Like Sherlock Holmes, you will really have to notice what you see.

By the end of this section, you should be able to:

- find an implied main idea
- identify an implied cause or effect
- distinguish between logical and emotional arguments
- determine the theme of a piece of literature

You'll look at different kinds of texts, including some poetry. The final lesson will then help you pull together everything from this section and from the rest of the book.

L·E·S·S·O·N

FINDING AN IMPLIED MAIN IDEA

16

LESSON SUMMARY
This lesson shows you how to find the main idea when there's no topic sentence or thesis statement to guide you.

Oh, the power of suggestion! Advertisers know it well—and so do writers. They know they can get an idea across without directly saying it. They know that they don't always need a topic sentence because they can use structure and language to *suggest* their ideas.

Think back to Lesson 2 for a moment. What is a **main idea?** It is a claim (**an assertion**) *about* the subject of the passage. It's also the thought that holds the whole passage together. Thus, it must be general enough to include all of the ideas in the passage. Like a net, it holds everything together. Main ideas are often stated in topic sentences.

So far, most of the passages in this book have topic sentences. But you'll often come across passages (like the story "The Tryout") that *don't* have topic sentences. Writers often imply ideas instead of stating them directly. To *imply* means to hint or suggest. You'll need to use your powers of observation to determine their message.

How to Find an Implied Main Idea

When the main idea is implied, there's no topic sentence, so finding the main idea requires some good detective work. But you already know the importance of structure, word choice, style, and tone. You know how to read carefully and find clues, and you know that these clues will help you figure out the main idea.

For example, take a look at the following paragraph:

> One of my summer reading books was *The Windows of Time*. Though it's more than 100 pages long, I read it in one afternoon. I couldn't wait to see what happened to Evelyn, the main character. But by the time I got to the end, I wondered if I should have spent my afternoon doing something else. The ending was so awful that I completely forgot I'd enjoyed most of the book.

There's no topic sentence here, but you should still be able to find the main idea. Look carefully at what the writer says and how she says it. What is she suggesting?

a. *The Windows of Time* is a terrific novel.
b. *The Windows of Time* is disappointing.
c. *The Windows of Time* is full of suspense.
d. *The Windows of Time* is a lousy novel.

The correct answer is (b)—the novel is disappointing. How can you tell that this is the main idea? First, we can eliminate choice (c), because it's too specific to be a main idea. It deals only with one specific aspect of the novel (its suspense).

Sentences (a), (b), and (d), on the other hand, all express a larger idea—a general assertion about the quality of the novel. But only one of these statements can actually serve as a "net" for the whole paragraph. Notice that while the first few sentences *praise* the novel, the last two *criticize* it. (The word "but" at the beginning of the third sentence signals that the positive review is going to turn negative.) Clearly, this is a mixed review. Therefore, the best answer is (b). Sentence (a) is too positive and doesn't account for the "awful" ending. Sentence (d), on the other hand, is too negative and doesn't account for the suspense and interest in the main character. But Sentence (b) allows for both positive and negative—when a good thing turns bad, we often feel disappointed.

Now let's look at another example. Here, the word choice will be more important, so read carefully.

> Fortunately, none of Toby's friends had ever seen the apartment where Toby lived with his mother and sister. Sandwiched between two burnt-out buildings, his two-story apartment building was by far the ugliest one on the block. It was a real eyesore: peeling orange paint (orange!), broken windows, crooked steps, crooked everything. He could just imagine what his friends would say if they ever saw this poor excuse for a building.

Which of the following expresses the main idea of this paragraph?

a. Toby wishes he could move to a nicer building.
b. Toby wishes his dad still lived with them.
c. Toby is glad none of his friends know where he lives.
d. Toby is sad because he doesn't have any friends.

From the description, we can safely assume that Toby doesn't like his apartment building and wishes he could move to a nicer building (a). But that idea isn't general enough to cover the whole paragraph, because it doesn't say anything about his friends. Sentence (d) is about his building, so it's not broad enough either. Besides, the first sentence states that Toby *has* friends. We know that Toby lives only with his mother and little sister, so we might *assume* that he wishes his dad still lived with them (b). But there's nothing in the paragraph to support that assumption, and this idea doesn't include the two main topics of the paragraph—Toby's building and Toby's friends.

What the paragraph adds up to is that Toby is terribly embarrassed about his building, and he's glad none of his friends have seen it (c). This is the main idea. The paragraph opens with the word "fortunately," so we know that he thinks it's a good thing none of them have been there. Plus, look at the word choice. Notice how the building is described. It's "by far the ugliest on the block," which is saying a lot since it's stuck between two burnt-out buildings. The writer calls it an "eyesore," and repeats "orange" with an exclamation point to emphasize how ugly the color is. Everything's "crooked" in this "poor excuse for a building." He's ashamed of where he lives and worries about what his friends would think if they saw it.

EXERCISE 1
Questions
Read the paragraphs below and circle the letter of the answer you think is correct.

1. Day after day, Johnny chooses to sit at his computer instead of going outside with his friends. A few months ago, he'd get half a dozen phone calls from his friends every night. Now, he might get one or two a week. Used to be his friends would come over two, three days a week after school. Now, he spends his afternoons alone with his computer.

   The main idea is:

   a. Johnny and his friends are all spending time with their computers instead of one another.
   b. Johnny's friends aren't very good friends.
   c. Johnny has alienated his friends by spending so much time on the computer.
   d. Johnny and his friends prefer to communicate by computer.

2. We've had Ginger since I was two years old. Every morning, she wakes me up by licking my cheek. That's her way of telling me she's hungry. When she wants attention, she'll weave in and out of my legs and meow until I pick her up and hold her. And I can always tell when Ginger wants to play. She'll bring me her toys and will keep dropping them (usually right on my homework!) until I stop what I'm doing and play with her for a while.

   A good topic sentence for this paragraph would be:

   a. I take excellent care of Ginger.
   b. Ginger is a demanding pet.
   c. Ginger and I have grown up together.
   d. Ginger is good at telling me what she wants.

CASTING A NET

When you're looking for an implied main idea, what you're really doing is searching for the right "net" to cast over the passage. What is the idea that encompasses all of the other ideas in the passage? What holds it together? (Remember, a paragraph, by definition, is a group of sentences about the same idea.)

What if you're looking for the main idea of *several* paragraphs? Well, it's really the same thing. Instead of determining the main idea of an individual paragraph, you're determining the overall main idea. Remember the comparison between a table and an essay? In an essay, the overall main idea is the tabletop while the supporting ideas are the legs that hold up (support) the table. Each of those legs, though, might be paragraphs of their own with their own main idea and supporting sentences.

Here's a very short essay with an implied main idea. Read it carefully. Can you see what the whole passage adds up to?

It has been more than 25 years since the National Aeronautic and Space Administration (NASA) last sent a craft to land on the moon. A lunar prospector took off in January 1998, in the first moon shot since astronauts last walked on the moon in 1972. This time, the moon-traveler is only a low-cost robot that will spend a year on the surface of the moon, collecting minerals and ice.

Unlike the moon shots of the 1960s and 1970s, the lunar prospector does not carry a camera, so the American public will not get to see new pictures of the moon's surface. Instead, the prospector carries instruments that will map the makeup of the entire surface of the moon.

Scientists are anxious for the results of the entire mission and of one exploration in particular—that done by the neutron spectrometer. Using this instrument, the prospector will examine the moon's poles, searching for signs of water ice. There has long been speculation that frozen water from comets may have accumulated in craters at one of the moon's poles and may still be there, as this pole is permanently shielded from the sun.

Which of the following seems to best express the overall main idea of this passage?

a. There is a great deal we can learn from studying the moon.
b. The prospector will collect surface data rather than take pictures.
c. NASA's newest moon-traveler is on an important mission.
d. Scientists hope the prospector will return with evidence of water on the moon.

If you remember that a main idea must be general enough to hold the whole passage together *and* that a main idea must also be an assertion about the subject, then it should be pretty easy to tell which is the correct answer. First, answers (b) and (d) are too specific to be the main idea; they deal only with information in the second and third paragraphs, respectively. Second, they state only facts; they don't make an assertion about the subject. They can't be the overall main idea for this passage.

Answers (a) and (c), on the other hand, both make assertions about the subject and are general. Notice how they both allow room for detailed support. But while (a) casts a wide enough net, it's not the right net for this passage. The passage is about what NASA hopes to learn from *this* specific mission. So while (b) and (d) are too specific, (a) is too general to be the main idea of this passage. "NASA's newest moon-traveler is on an important mission," however, casts a net that's just the right size.

EXERCISE 2

Read the following passage carefully and actively. Then circle the answers of the questions that follow.

A healthy diet with proper nutrition is essential for maintaining good overall health. Since vitamins were discovered early in the twentieth century, people have routinely been taking vitamin supplements for this purpose. The Recommended Daily Allowance (RDA) is a frequently used nutritional standard for maintaining optimal health.

The RDA specifies the recommended amount of a number of nutrients for people in many different age and gender groups. With RDA, consumers can see how much of those nutrients are offered in the products they buy and can better plan for a nutritious meal. But RDA values are based on the assumption that it is possible to accurately define nutritional requirements for a given group. In reality, individual nutritional requirements can vary widely within each group.

The efficiency with which a person converts food into nutrients can also vary widely. Certain foods when eaten in combination actually prevent the absorption of nutrients. For example, spinach combined with milk reduces the amount of calcium available to the body from the milk, but this is not reflected in RDA values.

The RDA approach also specifies a different dietary requirement for each age and gender. However, it is clearly unrealistic to expect a homemaker to prepare a different menu for each family member.

Questions

1. Which of the following sentences best expresses the overall main idea of this passage?
   a. Still, although we cannot rely solely upon RDA to ensure our overall long-term health, it can be a useful guide.
   b. The RDA approach is problematic and should be avoided.
   c. It's important for consumers to monitor RDA levels carefully.
   d. After all, vitamins are the most important part of a healthy diet.

2. Where would this overall main idea make the most sense in the passage?
   a. at the beginning of the first paragraph
   b. at the end of the first paragraph
   c. at the beginning of the last paragraph
   d. at the end of the last paragraph

SUMMARY

Writers often *suggest* their main idea without actually *saying* it. (This is especially true in literature, as you'll see in Lesson 19.) Finding an implied main idea takes extra careful detective work. Look for clues in what the writer says and how he or she says it. Consider the structure, the point of view, word choice, style, and tone. What does the passage add up to? What assertion can you make that holds together all of the ideas in that passage?

Skill Building until Next Time

1. Listen carefully to people today. Do they sometimes suggest things without actually saying them? Are there times when you use suggestion to express your ideas? How do you do this?

2. Write a paragraph that does not have a topic sentence. Start with a clear main idea, but don't write that main idea down. Then, put in clues that will help readers figure out your main idea. For example, make a claim about yourself. What kind of person are you? Keep that main idea in your head. Next, write several sentences that support your assertion. Make sure those sentences lead your reader to your main idea. Then show your paragraph to others. Can they determine the main idea from what you've written?

ANSWERS

EXERCISE 1

1. c. By comparing and contrasting how things used to be to how they are now, we can see that Johnny's choice (to "sit at his computer instead of going outside with his friends") has created a distance between them. They don't call or come by as they used to. Choice (a) is incorrect because we don't know from the paragraph whether Johnny's friends are doing the same thing or not. It's possible, but remember there must be evidence in the passage to support a main idea. There is no mention in this passage about how Johnny's friends spend their time, or that they prefer to communicate by computer (d). Choice (b) is also incorrect because it's clear that Johnny is choosing his computer over his friends. He's the one who's not being a good friend.

2. d. The writer may indeed take very good care of Ginger (a), but that's not the main idea here. Each specific example in this paragraph is about how Ginger communicates her desires to the writer.

EXERCISE 2

1. a. Each paragraph in this passage deals with the RDA and its values, so choice (d) is incorrect. Choice (b) is incorrect because paragraph two mentions two specific benefits of RDA. Choice (c) is incorrect because it is too specific.

2. d. The best place for this overall main idea would be the very end of the passage. The passage explains what the RDA is, how it helps us, and why it is problematic. It can then conclude with this main idea—that while there are problems with the RDA, it's still a helpful guide.

L·E·S·S·O·N

ASSUMING CAUSES AND PREDICTING EFFECTS

17

LESSON SUMMARY

Sometimes, writers don't directly explain a cause or effect. Instead, they *suggest* it. This lesson shows you how to "read between the lines" and find implied causes and effects.

Sometimes, we want to say something, but we don't want to just "tell it like it is." So, like writers, we use suggestion to get our point across. In the previous lesson, you saw how writers can use suggestion to convey their main idea. But suggestion works at all levels; supporting ideas and even specific details can be implied, too. This lesson focuses on two specific types of suggestion: implied cause and implied effect.

First, here's a quick review. A **cause** is a person or thing that makes something happen. An **effect** is the change created by an action or cause. Cause tells you why something happened; effect tells you what happened as a result of that action.

FINDING IMPLIED CAUSE

Imagine that you have a classmate named Len. He walks into the room and looks upset. You know he has just met with the principal. You know that he's been late for school a lot lately and that he's been cutting classes. You also know that Len's parents would go crazy if they knew what Len was doing. When Len walks into the room, he doesn't say anything to you. But you can guess why he's upset:

a. He has to do extra assignments to make up for being late.
b. He is going to be transferred to another class.
c. He's just found out the principal has told his parents.

From what you know, it makes sense to conclude that Len is upset because (C), the principal has reported Len's behavior to his parents. Len doesn't tell you this, but that's what the "clues" add up to. You used what you know about Len, his parents, and the principal to figure out the cause of Len's distress.

You can use the same process to determine an implied cause when you read. Here's how Len's problem might look in a reading passage:

Len was late for school for the ninth time in three weeks. In the last month, he'd cut Biology five times and Social Studies twelve times. His parents would ground him for life if they knew he'd been skipping classes. He looked nervous when he was called to the principal's office. A few minutes later, when he came back, he looked extremely upset. He walked past his classmates without saying a word and put his head down on the desk.

On a reading test, you might be asked to identify why Len is upset. This question asks you to identify the cause. Again, the clues add up to one thing: That Len's parents have been informed of his behavior.

Writers suggest cause in many ways. In the passage above, the clues are mostly action clues—what people said and did. Clues can also come in the form of details, word choice, and style. For example, look at the following passage:

Dennis was scared—really scared. His knees were weak. He looked down, 20 feet, to the water below. He looked up again, quickly. He tried to think of something else. He tried to reassure himself. "It's only 20 feet!" he said aloud. But that only made it sound worse. Twenty feet! He felt dizzy and hot.

This writer could have simply said, "Dennis was scared. He was afraid of heights." Instead, she *suggests* the cause of Dennis's fear by *showing* you how Dennis feels. This way, you are able to see for yourself what Dennis is going through. And through these details, you can conclude that he is afraid of heights. The repetition of "20 feet" is another clue, and so is the sentence structure. Notice that the sentences are short and choppy. In fact, they sound a little panicky. This helps to reflect how Dennis feels.

EXERCISE 1

Below is an excerpt from a short story. Read the passage carefully, and then circle the answers of the questions that follow.

Anne sat with her feet up on the couch, drinking a Coke. She heard footsteps by the front door. Brenda was right on time, as usual. Never a minute early or late—for her, everything was very exact.

Anne placed her feet on the floor, reached for the remote and turned off the television. She knew Brenda would demand her complete attention. She knew Brenda would hang up her coat in the closet by the door (third hanger from the left) and then head to the kitchen for her daily inspection (exactly seven steps). She knew this because they had been roommates for six months. Taking a deep breath, she thought about what she would say to Brenda. She waited and watched from her spot on the couch.

A moment later, Brenda stepped into the kitchen and surveyed the scene. Anne watched her expression, watched her eyes focus on the sink, and watched her face sadden when she saw the dishes piled high. Looking at the dishes, Brenda said disappointedly, "I don't believe what I'm seeing. I thought we agreed to share the responsibilities. I thought it was your turn to clean the kitchen this week."

"I haven't gotten to them yet," Anne replied. "I've been busy. Relax. I've got all night." She walked into the kitchen and added her empty glass to the top of the pile.

Brenda fumed. "You know I'm having company tonight! Somehow I thought you would have done your share in the kitchen. If we want to remain roommates, things have to change. "

The phone rang, and Anne darted to answer it.

Brenda said in the background, "Anne, please tell them to call back, we need to settle this now. I told you I'm having company soon."

Anne ignored Brenda's comment and continued to engage in conversation with a good friend of hers. "Did I ever tell you about the time when. . . . "

Questions

Circle the letter of the correct answer.

1. Why does Brenda get angry?
   a. because Anne is unfriendly.
   b. because she had a bad day at work.
   c. because Anne didn't do the dishes.
   d. because Anne is lazy.

2. Why didn't Anne do the dishes?
   a. because she didn't have time to do them.
   b. because she wanted to start a fight.
   c. because she was too lazy.
   d. because she wants Brenda to get a new roommate.

3. What does Anne do that shows she doesn't intend to shoulder her share of the responsibilities?
   a. She turns off the television.
   b. She begins to wash the dishes in the sink.
   c. She always helps around the house.
   d. She talks on the phone with a good friend.

FINDING IMPLIED EFFECTS

Just as writers can imply cause, they can also suggest effects. In the practice passage you just read, Anne clearly had a specific goal. She purposely decided not to do the dishes in an act of rebellion. Why? You know a little bit about Anne and Brenda from the passage. Use that knowledge to answer the following question. What do you think Anne was hoping to achieve? What effect do you think she was looking for?

a. that Brenda would do the dishes herself for once
b. that Brenda would get herself a new roommate
c. that Brenda would stop being so neat and so regimented

How can you tell that (c) is the best answer? You have to look carefully at the passage. Anne says, "Relax. I've got all night." But, Brenda has her own priorities. She says she is expecting company. Anne responds by ignoring her and turning to a phone conversation.

The passage doesn't directly say so, but from these clues, you can conclude that Anne's personality is clearly more relaxed than Brenda's. That's why she didn't do the dishes and that's also why she gladly took a phone call.

But will she get the effect she hoped for? Take another look at the passage, paying close attention to the end. What do you think? Will Anne get her wish? Will Brenda change her ways? Why do you think so?

Most likely, Anne won't get her wish. How can you tell? The end of the passage offers a strong clue. Brenda clearly wants to resolve the situation, but she can't compete with the telephone and probably not with Anne's relaxed personality.

EXERCISE 2

Imagine that there has been a robbery in your apartment building. The victim is Mr. Ash, who lives a few doors down the hall. Below are two passages. One is a statement by the building manager, Mr. Billings. The other is a statement from Ms. Wilkins, who lives next door to Mr. Ash. Read their statements carefully and answer the question that follows. Use their statements to predict some effects. What will happen as a result of the robbery?

> **Mr. Billings (building manager):** This is the third robbery this month. Each time, thieves have gotten past building security. Each time, the thieves stole everything in the victim's apartment. Yet each time, the security officers claim they didn't see anything unusual.

> **Ms. Wilkins (Mr. Ash's neighbor):** Well, Mr. Ash is a carefree man. I knock on his door and he hollers, "Come in!" I just push the door open because it's never locked. He often forgets things, too. He forgets where he parked his car or where he put his keys. One time, I found him in the hall searching through his bags. He couldn't find his keys, but it didn't matter; the door was open anyway. And he left it open the day he was robbed. He's really shaken up by this. He says he can't trust anybody anymore.

Questions

Which of the following are likely to happen as a result of the robbery? What *effects* do these statements suggest? Circle the numbers of the correct answers.

1. Building security will be tightened.

2. Tenants will have to notify security before moving furniture out of the building.

3. The security officers will be fired.

4. The security officers will be thoroughly questioned.

5. Security cameras will be installed throughout the building.

6. Mr. Ash will get his things back.

7. Mr. Ash will be more careful with his keys.

8. Mr. Ash will get new locks on his door.

9. Mr. Ash will keep his door locked.

10. Some tenants will move out of the building.

SUMMARY

Writers will often suggest causes and effects without explicitly stating them. You can use clues in the text to uncover these implied ideas. These clues can come in the form of action (what people say or do), specific details, word choice, tone, and style. Active readers look carefully at what people say and do and pay particular attention to details, word choice, and tone. By adding up these clues, they can determine implied cause and effect.

> ## Skill Building until Next Time
>
> 1. Watch people today and observe how they are behaving. Do they seem happy? Sad? Angry? See if you can guess the cause of their emotion or behavior. What clues can you uncover? Are they reading a letter? Talking with someone? Waiting for something? *Why* might they be acting this way? For example, if you see a man at a bus stop pacing back and forth and checking his watch every 30 seconds, you can infer that the bus is late or that he's late for an appointment.
> 2. Read a news article today. Choose one that's about a current event like an election or a scientific discovery. What effects do you think will result from this event? Come up with at least three effects. Be sure that you can support your predictions with evidence from the article.

ANSWERS

EXERCISE 1

1. c. Brenda's face "hardens" with anger when she sees the dishes in the sink. You can tell she expects the kitchen to be clean when she comes home. Anne waits for Brenda to begin her "daily inspection," and when she walks in, she looks around the kitchen as if she's inspecting it. Then she sees the dishes and her face hardens. She asks why the dishes are still in the sink. Further, she reminds Anne about the company she is expecting.

2. b. You can tell Anne is not worried about Brenda's reaction because she is lazily watching television instead of cleaning the kitchen. She knows Brenda is going to check the kitchen and that Brenda is going to be mad about the dishes when she sees them. As Anne waits, she thinks about what she is going to say to Brenda.

3. d. Anne's actions speak loudly. She answers the phone and discontinues a conversation that is important if the two of them intend to remain roommates.

EXERCISE 2

1, 2, 4, 5, 7 and 9 are all logical effects to predict from these statements. Effect 3 is not likely; it's too extreme. The building manager's statement doesn't suggest that the security officers will be fired, but it *does* suggest that he plans to look into the problem. That's why 4 is a logical outcome. Nothing in either statement suggests that Mr. Ash will get his things back. In fact, there's no mention at all of what was stolen. Mr. Ash left the door open while he was robbed, so there's no need for him to get new locks. But you *can* conclude that Mr. Ash will be more careful. Finally, there's no suggestion that tenants plan to move. In fact, if they know security will be improved, they'd be more likely to want to stay.

L·E·S·S·O·N

EMOTIONAL VERSUS LOGICAL APPEALS

LESSON SUMMARY

When writers want to convince, they can use both logic and emotion to persuade. This lesson explains the difference between logical and emotional appeals so you can better recognize a good argument.

Imagine you are about to do something when suddenly someone shouts, "You can't do that!"

"Why not?" you ask.

"Because!"

Now, "because!" isn't a very satisfactory answer because it doesn't give you a **reason** to stop doing what you're doing. And because it doesn't give you a good reason, it's not a convincing or *reasonable* argument. An **argument** is a claim supported by reasons or evidence. Here's an example of a simple argument:

You should bring your umbrella. It's going to rain.

In this argument, the first sentence, "You should bring your umbrella," is the main claim. Its aim is to get you to think or act in a certain way. The second sentence provides a specific **reason** for accepting that claim—it tells you *why* you should bring your umbrella.

Here's another brief argument:

Let's go to Denny's Pizza, not Joe's. Denny's has an after-school special for students—a large pie for $5.00!

This argument also begins with a claim that tries to convince you to do something (go to Denny's Pizza, not Joe's). The second sentence provides a *reason* for going to Denny's instead of Joe's (the after-school special).

As you can see from these two arguments, **reason** is a key word. Reason has two meanings:

Reason
1. A motive, grounds, or cause for something. Example: *He had a good reason to quit his job.*
2. Good sense or judgment. Example: *She made a very reasonable decision.*

An argument, then, offers *reasons* for accepting its claim. In a good argument, those reasons are *reasonable.* They're based on evidence or good sense or judgment.

EMOTIONAL AND LOGICAL APPEALS

The goal of an argument is to convince others to accept your claim. To do this, you can use two approaches: You can appeal to **logic,** or you can appeal to **emotions.** The difference between these two kinds of appeals is important. Sometimes, writers will rely *only* on appeals to emotion; they won't provide any real *evidence* for why you should believe what they say. They know that feelings are powerful, and they know it's easy for readers to get caught up in their emotions. They usually hope to get you so angry, or so scared, or so excited that you will

forget to look for a sense of reason in their arguments. Thus, you need to be able to recognize **emotional** appeals so you can look beyond them for a **logical** argument.

Of course, emotional appeals can *strengthen* an argument, and most writers will use a combination of emotional and logical appeals. But an argument shouldn't rely on emotional appeals alone. A good argument must be based in logic. Otherwise, it lacks good sense.

Logical: According to reason; according to conclusions drawn from evidence or good common sense.
Emotional: Drawn from the emotions, from intense mental feelings.

An emotional appeal is support for an argument that is based on feelings and emotions. Logical appeals, on the other hand, are supporting ideas based on reason, evidence, or common sense. Here's an example. Look at the claim below. Then, read the logical and emotional appeals that follow:

Claim:	We should go to Denny's Pizza instead of Joe's.
Logical appeal:	Denny's has an after-school pizza special.
Emotional appeal:	Only losers go to Joe's.

The logical appeal is one that's based on reason. It makes good sense to go to the pizzeria that offers students a price break (unless, of course, the pizza is really lousy). The emotional appeal, on the other hand, doesn't offer a logical reason. It tries to convince you not to go to Joe's by making you want to fit in. It appeals to your desire to belong, your fear of being labeled a loser, instead of dealing with logical issues, such as cost, location, or taste.

AN EMOTIONAL ARGUMENT

Here's a short argument that relies mostly on emotion to convince. Read it carefully and actively. Notice how you feel as you read. Is the writer trying to make you angry? Sad? How does the writer try to make you feel about hunters? Does the writer offer any logical appeals to support her argument?

Abolish Hunting!
Hunting should be abolished! For one thing, hunting is not a "sport," as so many people like to call it. For another, poor, defenseless animals have just as much a right to live as people do. What right do hunters have to take an animal's life just for "sport"? None! Further, most hunters don't even use the animals for food. They should be ashamed of such cruelty!

Even though you may find this argument convincing, you have to admit that there's no real *logic* in this argument. This writer relies solely on emotional appeals (and circular reasoning) to convince you that hunting should be abolished.

Let's take a closer look to see how this works. In the first paragraph, the writer begins by claiming that hunting "is not a 'sport.'" But she does not explain *why* it's not a sport. Instead, she tries to make us feel outraged because poor, defenseless animals are being killed. But notice that she hasn't explained *why* it's not a sport. She hasn't offered any logical reasons for why it should be abolished.

Next, the writer claims that animals have "just as much a right to live as people do." But she doesn't explain why they have just as much a right. Instead, she

asks a question that really just restates her claim. She also uses the words "poor" and "defenseless" to describe animals. Here, her goal is to make us feel pity for the animals and anger toward the hunters.

The rest of the paragraph deals with the issue of hunters not eating the animals they kill. Again, the language the writer uses is designed to make us angry with hunters, to make us feel as if the hunters are heartless, horrible people. Unfortunately, she never offers a *logical* reason to abolish hunting.

Another clue, by the way, that this argument is too emotional is the number of exclamation points. You can see that the writer feels very passionately about her subject by how often she uses exclamation points. Being passionate about a subject is not in itself a bad thing; but when we're too emotional, sometimes we forget to back up those emotions with logic.

ADDING LOGIC

Emotional appeals can be very convincing, but a good argument doesn't rely just on this technique. A good argument will always be grounded in logical appeals. What sort of logical appeals might this writer have used instead of—or at least *in addition* to—all of these emotional appeals? Here are a few possibilities:

Hunting should be abolished because:

1. It is a sport that might put guns into the hands of young children.
2. Dozens of people are injured and even killed each year in hunting accidents.
3. Most people don't need to kill animals for food. There are plenty of grocery stores to buy food.

Conversely, one might make the following logical appeals to argue that hunting should *not* be abolished:

Hunting is an important tool in animal population control. Without hunting, some animals (such as deer) would overpopulate in areas that can't support a large population. Instead of a quick death from hunting, they'd die slowly in the agony of starvation.

A LOGICAL ARGUMENT

Here's an argument that's much better than the first. You don't have to agree with the writer to see that this argument is much stronger. This author doesn't appeal just to your emotions; instead, she bases her arguments in logic. Read the passage carefully and actively.

Recycle!

It's not only *right* to recycle, it's our *duty*. In nature, everything is recycled. A dead animal, for example, is food for many levels in the food chain; it even feeds organisms in the soil. Nothing is wasted. But humans have created things like plastic that can't be broken down by nature. In other words, we've created permanent litter. Our trash kills animals and pollutes water and soil, and if we continue to let it pile up, we may eventually have a trash mess that's out of control. If nature can't reuse it, we must recycle it. We've made a mess, and we should clean it up—because nature can't.

Recycling is also the right thing to do for another reason. The earth is rich in resources, but its supply of materials is not endless. We use up our resources much faster than the earth is able to replenish them. For example, each year we cut down approximately four million acres of timber. But it takes an average of 25 years for replacement trees to mature. Recycling can

help us reduce the risk of using up our natural resources.

This writer doesn't try to convince you by rousing your emotions. Instead, he shows you how logical it is to recycle. First, the writer points out that nature recycles everything, but that humans have created trash that nature can't recycle. It makes good common sense—it's good judgment—to argue that if nature can't recycle it, we should. The second appeal is also very logical. If we don't recycle, we will eventually run out of resources. This makes sense, and the author provides specific evidence to support this claim. Because this argument is so logical, it's very convincing.

EXERCISE 1

Read the passages below carefully. Does the writer appeal to your emotions, or does the writer use logic (common sense, reason, or evidence) to convince you?

Questions

Write an E in the blank if the passage appeals to your emotions and an L if it appeals to logic.

_____ **1.** You *have* to get the new U2 CD! The songs are great, and it's on sale right now at The Wiz.

_____ **2.** You *have* to get the new U2 CD! That is, if you're not too busy listening to the junk you normally listen to.

_____ **3.** Ed, can you help me with my homework tonight? You're such a pal!

_____ **4.** Ed, can you help me with my homework tonight? I know you got straight A's in algebra and understand it.

____ **5.** Ed, can you help me with my math home-work tonight? In turn, I'll help you with your essay.

____ **6.** Ed, can you help me with my homework tonight? You're the smartest guy I know.

____ **7.** Let's go to the beach tomorrow. It's going to be 100° and humid.

____ **8.** Let's go to the beach tomorrow. I'd like to get some sun.

EXERCISE 2

Here's another set of sentences. This time, they're not paired together, so you'll need to pay extra attention to each one. Read them carefully. Does the writer appeal to your emotions, or is the author using logic (common sense, reason, or evidence)?

Questions

Write an E in the blank if the passage appeals to your emotions. Write an L if it appeals to logic.

____ **1.** Year-round school is a good idea. Students wouldn't have to spend the first month of school reviewing everything they'd forgotten over the summer.

____ **2.** Every school should have metal detectors. How do you know your classmates aren't bringing guns to school?

____ **3.** Young children shouldn't watch TV. They need to interact with others, and TV is too passive.

____ **4.** Come on, you try. We all did.

____ **5.** Join the track team with me. We're both good runners and it'll be fun to train and to compete.

____ **6.** Don't say a word to Mom and Dad—or you'll regret it!

SUMMARY

Good arguments offer readers logical reasons for accepting their claims—reasons based on evidence or good common sense. Arguments can also appeal to your emotions. They may try to make you feel angry or scared, flattered or not part of the crowd. While our feelings are important, it's often dangerous to rely only on emotions when judging an argument. When you read, check to see that there's also *logic* behind an argument.

Skill Building until Next time

- Listen closely to people as they try to convince you (or others) to do something. Do they appeal to logic or to emotions?
- Make an argumentative (debatable) claim, such as "Music should be free to download from the Internet." Then offer a logical appeal and an emotional appeal for that claim.

ANSWERS

EXERCISE 1

1. L
2. E
3. E
4. L
5. L
6. E
7. L
8. L

EXERCISE 2

1. L
2. E. This argument tries to convince you by frightening you.
3. L
4. E. This is plain old peer pressure—a very common emotional appeal.
5. L
6. E. This argument tries to scare you into keeping quiet, but it doesn't give you a logical reason for doing so.

L·E·S·S·O·N

UNCOVERING MEANING IN LITERATURE

19

LESSON SUMMARY

This lesson will show you how to find meaning in literature. You'll learn how to look for clues to find theme in stories, poems, and plays.

Many people are intimidated by **literature.** That's understandable because in literature, writers don't come right out and tell you the main idea. You have to somehow figure out what idea the author is trying to convey. But finding the main idea or **theme** in literature isn't so different from finding the main idea in other texts. If you look carefully for clues, you can uncover meaning in literature.

Literature includes short stories, novels, poems, and plays. People often find poetry the hardest to understand, but you can find meaning in poems, too. All you have to do is read between the lines. This lesson will show you how.

MAIN IDEAS IN LITERATURE

Theme is the overall message or idea that the writer wants to convey. Like a main idea, the theme is different from subject in that the theme *says something about* the subject. For example, take John Donne's poem "Death Be Not

Proud." The *subject* of the poem is death. But the *theme* of the poem says something *about* death. The poem's message is that death is a gift for those who believe in God.

The main idea of a text is the thought that holds everything together. Likewise, the theme of a work of literature is the thought that holds together the characters and action. It's the idea that determines word choice, structure, and style.

To practice the skill of analyzing themes, this lesson introduces several poems. Reading poetry can be intimidating, but don't be frightened. You already have the skills you need to find meaning in poems. You just have to read a little more carefully and focus on using your observational skills. Pay close attention to word choice and to how the poems are organized. You find theme in poetry the same way you find it in other kinds of writing—by looking for clues in the action, in word choice, in style, and in structure.

ACTION AND THEME

Let's start with a poem that has a lot of action: "A Poison Tree," from William Blake's *Songs of Innocence and Experience*. It has four stanzas. A **stanza** is a group of lines in a poem, much as a paragraph is a group of lines in an essay or story.

Read the poem carefully and read it out loud, too, because poetry is meant to be *heard* as well as read. Read it actively—underline, circle, and write in the margins. Several words have been defined for you to the right of the poem.

A Poison Tree

1 I was angry with my friend:
2 I told my wrath, my wrath did end.   *wrath = anger*
3 I was angry with my foe: *foe = enemy*
4 I told it not, my wrath did grow.

5 And I water'd it in fears,
6 Night and morning with my tears;
7 And I sunned it with smiles,
8 And with soft deceitful wiles.   *deceitful = to make others believe what isn't true*
                                              wiles = trickery, deceit

9 And it grew both by day and night,
10 Till it bore an apple bright;
11 And my foe beheld it shine,   *beheld = saw*
12 And he knew that it was mine,

13 And into my garden stole
14 When the night had veil'd the pole;   *veil'd = hidden*
15 In the morning glad I see
16 My foe outstretch'd beneath the tree.

To understand Blake's theme, you need to look carefully at *what* happened and then look at *why* it happened. The poem is organized both chronologically and by cause and effect, so let's break down the action in the first stanza. Let's use the word "speaker" to refer to the narrator of the poem.

In the first four lines, Blake sets up two situations. First, the speaker is angry with his friend (line 1) and he tells his friend about it (line 2). As a result, the anger goes away (line 2—"my wrath did end"). But he acts differently with his enemy. He doesn't tell his foe about his anger (line 4), and as a result, the anger grows (line 4).

Now look at the second stanza. It's important to know what "it" refers to in line 5. What is "it"? Tears? Smiles? Wrath? Reread the first stanza carefully and then read the second stanza.

Poems are broken up into lines, which is one of the things that can make poetry scary. Sometimes ideas are carried from one line to another, so that the end of a line doesn't mean the end of a thought. A line is not always a sentence. Likewise, ideas can be carried from one stanza to the next. Here, "it" connects the first and second stanzas. "It" is the speaker's wrath. How can you tell? "Wrath" is the last thing mentioned in the first stanza.

In the second stanza, the speaker "water'd" his wrath in fears and "sunned" his wrath with smiles and wiles. How can this be? Can you water and sun your anger?

No, not *literally*. The difficulty and beauty of poetry lies in this kind of language. Blake isn't being literal here; rather he's drawing a comparison between the speaker's anger to something that grows with water and sun. It's like some kind of plant. How do you know exactly what it is? Blake tells you in two key places: in the title, and in the last line. The poem is called "A Poison Tree." "Tree" is mentioned again in the last line of the poem.

The kind of comparison is something you've seen before in Lesson 13—it's a **metaphor**. Try not to confuse this with the word **simile**. A **simile** is a comparison that uses the words *like* or *as*. A metaphor, on the other hand, makes the comparison *without* the words *like* or *as*. A simile, in other words, says that A is *like* B; a metaphor says that A *is* B. Here is an example of each:

Simile: Your eyes are *like* the deep blue sea.
Metaphor: Your eyes *are* the deep blue sea.

Pay close attention to similes and metaphors, because they are important clues to meaning. Blake, for example, could have compared the speaker's anger to anything, but he chose to compare it to a tree. Why?

Trees have deep, strong roots and often flower or bear fruit. (This tree bears an apple.) They need sun and water to grow. Keep these traits in mind as you work through the rest of the poem.

EXERCISE 1
Now that you've seen how to work through the first half of the poem, it's your turn to try.

Questions
Reread the entire poem from beginning to end and circle the letter of the correct answer.

1. In the third stanza, the foe
   a. grows his own apple tree.
   b. shines the speaker's apple.
   c. sees the speaker's apple.

2. In the fourth stanza, the foe
   a. sneaks into the speaker's garden at night.
   b. invites the speaker into his garden.
   c. attacks the speaker at night.

3. At the end of the poem, the foe
   a. is waiting to kill the speaker with an apple.
   b. has been killed by the poisonous apple.
   c. has been killed by the speaker.

Now you know what happens in the poem, but one important question remains. What does it all add up to? What does it mean? In other words, what is the theme?

Look again at the action. Cause and effect are central to the theme of this poem. What does the speaker do? He tells his friend about his anger. What *doesn't* the speaker do? He *doesn't* tell his enemy about his anger. What happens to his anger, then? It grows and grows and it offers fruit that tempts his enemy. And what happens to his enemy? He steals the apple, but it is the fruit of anger. It is poisonous and it kills him. Keep all of this in mind. Now, read the following questions and circle the answer you think is correct.

EXERCISE 2
Questions

1. Which sentence best summarizes the theme of the poem?
   a. Don't steal. It can kill you.
   b. Choose your enemies carefully.
   c. If you don't talk about your anger, it can be deadly.

Think about your answer and remember that a theme must be general. It should cover the whole work; it can't relate to just one piece of it. Does the answer you chose hold together the whole poem?

LANGUAGE, EMOTIONS, AND THEME

In many poems, the theme is an idea, while in others, the theme is an emotion. That is, the poet wants readers to feel an emotion very strongly. Poets can accomplish this through language.

Next is a poem called "The Eagle," written by Alfred, Lord Tennyson. It's a good example of how language can draw out strong feelings in the reader. Read the poem actively. Read it both silently and out loud.

The Eagle

1 He clasps the crag with crooked hands;   *clasp = grab; crag = steep, rugged rock*
2 Close to the sun in lonely lands,
3 Ringed with the azure world, he stands.
4 The wrinkled sea beneath him crawls;
5 He watches from his mountain walls,
6 And like a thunderbolt he falls.

What do you notice about the language in this poem? Did you hear the rhyme in each stanza? Look at the last word in each line: *hands, lands, stands; crawls, walls,* and *falls.* Did you notice the repetition of sounds? Read the first line out loud again. Do you hear the repetition of the *k* sound? "He clasps the crag with crooked hands." This repetition of sound is called **alliteration.** Alliteration helps create mood in a poem and enables the poem to "make music." It's one of the favorite tools of poets.

There's another poetic tool in this poem. The poet says that the eagle ("he") "clasps" the rock "with crooked hands." Do eagles have hands? No, they don't. The poet has given the eagle human features. Poets often give animals or things human characteristics. This is called **personification.** Personification helps you *see* what the poet is describing.

EXERCISE 3

You've learned about several important poetic tools, including similes, metaphors, alliteration and personification.

Questions

Now, reread "The Eagle" carefully and actively. Circle the answer you think is correct.

1. Line 1 of the poem uses alliteration. Which other line uses alliteration?
   a. line 2
   b. line 3
   c. line 6

2. Line 1 also uses personification. Which other line uses personification?
   a. line 2
   b. line 4
   c. line 6

3. The last line of the poem reads, "And like a thunderbolt he falls." Which tool does this line use?
   a. personification
   b. metaphor
   c. simile

4. The poem compares the eagle to a thunderbolt. How do you think the speaker feels about eagles?
   a. They are weak, shy animals.
   b. They are fast, powerful animals.
   c. They are unpredictable, wild animals.

5. By the end of the poem, readers should feel a certain way about eagles. They should
   a. have great respect for eagles.
   b. be glad there aren't any eagles around.
   c. feel sorry for eagles.

ACTION + LANGUAGE = THEME

You've read a poem that uses mostly action and one that uses mostly language to convey theme. Now, here's a poem by the American writer Stephen Crane that combines both. Read it actively, looking carefully at the action and the language (word choice, style, and tone) of the poem. Read it out loud at least once.

A Man Said to the Universe

A man said to the universe:
"Sir, I exist!"
"However," replied the universe,
"The fact has not created in me
A sense of obligation."

Look carefully at the language in the poem. What kinds of words has the poet chosen? Are they warm, friendly words, or are they cold, distancing words? Do they make you feel comfortable, welcome? Or uncomfortable, rejected? Are they specific or general? Do you feel like there's a personal relationship here? Or are things formal, official?

Crane's word choice helps convey his theme. The words "sir," "fact," and "obligation" are cold and formal. There's no sense of personal relationship between the man and the universe. This is heightened by the general nature of the poem. It's just "a man"—not anyone specific, not anyone you know. Not anyone the universe knows, either. It's also written in the third-person point of view. The poem would have a different effect if it began, "I said to the universe."

Now read the poem again. Then answer the questions in Exercise 4.

EXERCISE 4
Questions

Circle the letter of the answer you think is correct.

1. What is the tone of the poem?
   a. warm, caring
   b. hot, angry
   c. cold, uncaring

2. What is the theme of the poem?
   a. The universe is too big for humans
   b. The universe is indifferent to humans
   c. Humans have no obligation to the universe

SUMMARY

You have the tools you need to find theme in literature; you just need to read actively and pay close attention to clues. Look closely at the action and the language. Watch for similes and metaphors, and think about the comparisons the writer is making. Enjoy the sound of alliteration and picture the image created by personification. Remember, poets choose their words carefully because they want to create a certain effect.

Skill Building until Next Time

- Read a poem on your own. Do you see any similes? Metaphors? Alliteration? Personification? Can you determine the tone? What happens? What does it add up to? What's the message?
- Read a short story today. Apply the technique you used to understand poems to determine the theme of the story.

ANSWERS

EXERCISE 1

1. c. See lines 10 and 11: "it bore an apple bright" / "my foe beheld it shine."

2. a. See line 13: "And into my garden stole."

3. b. You know the speaker's garden had a tree, and you know that this tree is a metaphor for the speaker's anger. You know that this tree had an apple, and you know that the poem is called "A Poison Tree." Finally, at the end of the poem, the foe is "outstretchd beneath the tree." What do all of these clues add up to? The foe snuck into the garden and ate the apple, but the apple was poisonous.

EXERCISE 2

1. c. Answer (c) best sums up the message or "lesson" of the poem. The speaker's anger vanished when he talked with his friend about it, but he does not talk about his anger with his enemy. Instead, he let it grow, and it became poisonous and deadly.

EXERCISE 3

1. a. Line 2 repeats the *l* sound in "lonely lands."

2. b. The sea "crawls" like a baby or a turtle.

3. c. Remember, a simile is a comparison using *like* or *as*. Here, the eagle is compared to a thunderbolt. This helps readers picture the eagle's flight. It also tells you something about the eagle—it's like an incredible force of nature.

4. b. Tennyson compares the eagle to a thunderbolt to show how powerful and fast eagles are.

5. a. People should feel great respect for eagles. This feeling is what the poem is all about.

EXERCISE 4

1. c. The words "sir," "fact," and "obligation" are cold and formal.

2. b. The universe says it does not feel an obligation and the tone is cold and uncaring. Further, the man also seems to be demanding attention from the universe. He yells, "Sir, I exist!" as if he wants the universe to pay attention to him. But the universe remains indifferent.

L·E·S·S·O·N

PUTTING IT ALL TOGETHER

20

SECTION SUMMARY

This lesson reviews Lessons 16–19 and pulls together what you've learned in this section. The practice exercises will also give you a chance to practice all of the skills you've learned throughout this book.

Congratulations, you've reached the final lesson in this book! This last chapter will briefly review Section Four and then give you two practice passages. These passages will require you to use skills from each of the four sections, so you'll have to think about the basics, structure and language, as well as strategies for reading between the lines. This might sound like a lot, but you'll probably be surprised by how easy it is to use all of these strategies at once. You started by building a strong foundation, and with each lesson, you've strengthened those basic skills and developed more advanced skills. Just remember to read actively and look for clues.

REVIEW: WHAT YOU'VE LEARNED

Here's a quick review of each lesson in this section:

Lesson 16: Finding an Implied Main Idea. You learned how to find the main idea in passages without topic sentences. You looked for clues in structure, language, and style. You learned how to find an idea that casts the right kind of "net" over the passage.

Lesson 17: Assuming Causes and Predicting Effects. You learned to "read between the lines" to find implied causes and effects. You looked for clues in action, structure, language, and style.

Lesson 18: Emotional versus Logical Appeals. You learned the difference between logical (based on reason) and emotional (based on feelings) appeals. You learned that while good arguments may rouse your emotions, they are based in logic.

Lesson 19: Uncovering Meaning in Literature. You learned that "theme" is the main idea or message in literature. You used clues in word choice, style, point of view, tone, structure, and action to find the themes in several poems. You learned to look for similes, metaphors, alliteration, and personification to help you find meaning.

In Section 1, you learned how to be an active reader, how to find the main idea, how to define words from context, and how to distinguish between fact and opinion. In Section 2, you learned about four main writing structures: chronological order, order of importance, comparison and contrast, and cause and effect. In Section 3, you learned how writers use point of view, word choice, style, and tone to help create meaning.

If any of these terms or strategies are unfamiliar, STOP. Take some time to review the term or strategy that is unclear.

SECTION 4 PRACTICE

Read these last practice passages actively and carefully. Then answer the questions that follow. (You might recognize the first and third paragraphs in Exercise 1 from Section 1.)

Note: If you come across unfamiliar words, do not look them up until *after* you've completed this practice exercise.

SECTION EXERCISE 1

For or Against?—That Is the Question
(1) Andy is the most unreasonable, pigheaded, subhuman life-form in the entire galaxy, and he makes me so angry I could scream! Of course, I love him like a brother. I sort of have to because he *is* my brother. More than that, he's my twin! That's right. Andy and Amy (that's me) have the same curly hair and dark eyes and equally stubborn temperaments. Yet, though we may look alike, on most issues we usually take diametrically opposite positions. If I say day, you can count on Andy to say night.

(2) Just this week, the big buzz in school was all about the PTA's proposal to adopt a school

dress code. Every student would be required to wear a uniform. Uniforms! Can you imagine? Oh, they won't be military-style uniforms, but the clothes would be uniform in color. The dress style would be sort of loose and liberal.

(3) Boys would wear white or blue button-down shirts, a school tie, blue or gray pants, and a navy blue blazer or cardigan sweater. Girls would wear white or blue blouses or sweaters, blue or gray pants or skirts, along with a navy blue blazer or cardigan sweater. Socks or tights could be black, gray, blue, or white. The teachers are divided: Some are in favor of the uniforms, others are opposed. The principal has asked the students to express their opinions by voting on the issue before making their decisions. She will have the final word on the dress code.

(4) I think a dress code is a good idea. The reason is simple. School is tough enough without worrying about looking cool every single day. The fact is, the less I have to decide first thing in the morning, the better. I can't tell you how many mornings I look into my closet and just stare, unable to decide what to wear. Of course, there are other mornings when my room looks like a cyclone had hit it, with bits and pieces of a dozen different possible outfits on the bed, on the floor, or dangling from the lamps. I also wouldn't mind not having to see guys wearing oversized jeans and shirts so huge they would fit a sumo wrestler. And I certainly would welcome not seeing kids showing off designer-labeled clothes.

(5) Andy is appalled at my opinion. He says he can't believe that I would be willing to give up my all-American teenage birthright by dressing like—well, like a typical teenager. Last night, he even dragged out Mom and Dad's high school photo albums. What a couple of peace-loving hippies they were!

(6) "Bruce Springsteen never wore a school uniform. Bob Dylan wouldn't have been caught dead in a school uniform!" he declared. Andy was now on his soapbox. "When I am feeling political, I want to be able to wear clothes made of natural, undyed fibers, sewn or assembled in countries that do not pollute the environment or exploit child labor. If I have to wear a uniform, I won't feel like me!"

(7) To which I replied, "So your personal heroes didn't wear school uniforms. Big deal! They went to high school about a million years ago! I feel sorry for you, brother dear. I had no idea that your ego is so fragile that it would be completely destroyed by gray or blue pants, a white or blue shirt, a tie, and a blazer."

(8) That really made him angry. Then he said, "You're just mimicking what you hear that new music teacher saying because you have a crush on him!"

(9) "That is so not true. He's just a very good teacher, that's all," I said, raising my voice in what mom would call "a very rude manner."

(10) "You have always been a stupid goody-two shoes, and you know it!" he snapped.

(11) "Is that so? Anyone who doesn't agree with you is automatically stupid. And that's the stupidest thing of all!" I said.

(12) Fortunately, the bell rang before we could do each other physical harm, and we went (thankfully) to our separate classes.

(13) The vote for or against uniforms took place later that day. The results of the vote and the principal's decision will be announced next week. I wonder what it will be. I know how I voted, and I'm pretty sure I know how Andy voted.

(14) How would you vote—for or against?

Questions

Read the following questions. Circle the letter of the answer you think is correct.

1. Amy and Andy fight because
   a. neither one is able to convince the other to change his or her point of view.
   b. they're both stubborn.
   c. they always take the opposite view on issues.
   d. they don't like each other very much.

2. You know that this selection is a personal narrative because the story is about a
   a. personal experience and is told in the first person.
   b. historical event and is told in the third person.
   c. conflict of opinions between two people.
   d. school policy decision that will affect many people.

3. Which of the following is the best statement of Andy's position on the issue presented in the story?
   a. School clothing should reflect parents' values.
   b. Wearing school uniforms means one less decision every morning.
   c. How one dresses should be an expression of one's personality.
   d. Teenagers should never follow the latest fads in dress.

4. Which of these statements from the story is a form of an emotional appeal?
   a. "The results of the vote and the principal's decision will be announced next week."
   b. "The teachers are divided; some are in favor of uniforms; others are opposed."
   c. "The big buzz in school was all about the PTA's proposal to adopt a school dress code."
   d. "Your ego is so fragile that it would be completely destroyed by gray or blue pants."

5. Amy's position on school uniforms is most likely based on
   a. logical conclusions drawn on her own observation and personal experience.
   b. an emotional response to what she has been told by people in authority.
   c. her preference for designer-labeled clothes.
   d. not liking anything her brother likes.

6. Is there enough information in this story to predict an outcome? If so, what will probably happen next in the story?
   a. Yes. Students, teachers, and all staff members will begin wearing uniforms.
   b. Yes. Students will vote against uniforms, and the principal will agree with their decision.
   c. Yes. Students will vote against uniforms, and the principal will disagree with their decision.
   d. No. There is no way to determine what the outcome will be.

7. Read the following sentences from the story:

   Andy is appalled at my opinion. He says he can't believe that I would be willing to give up my all-American teenage birthright by dressing like—well, like a typical teenager.

As it is used in these sentences, what does
appalled mean?

a. angry

b. in denial

c. supportive of

d. horrified by

8. The overall organizing principle of this passage
is

a. chronological.

b. order of importance.

c. comparison and contrast.

d. cause and effect.

9. Which of the following best expresses the main
point Amy is trying to make in paragraph 7?

a. Andy shouldn't look up to his heroes so much.

b. Our clothes shouldn't determine how we feel
about ourselves.

c. Andy needs more modern heroes.

d. Andy's lack of self-confidence is reflected in
his clothing.

EXERCISE 2

From *One Day of Life* by Manlio Argueta

My parents could send me only to the first
grade. Not because they didn't want to but
because we were so many at home and I was
the only girl, in charge of grinding corn and
cooking it and then taking tortillas to my brothers in the cornfields.

My brothers used to kill themselves chopping and hoeing. My father, too.

My mother and I would take care of the
house. All together there were fourteen of us—
I and my folks and eleven brothers—even after

three children had died. They died of dehydration. I remember how my father held the last one
by his feet so that blood would run to his head,
but nothing happened. He died with his head
caved in. All their heads sunk in after serious bouts
of diarrhea; once diarrhea begins there's no salvation. They all died before their first birthday.

Children die of dehydration only when
they're very little, since their bones are very soft,
and if you're not careful, they get diarrhea and
the forehead sinks in.

Children go to heaven. That's what the
priest used to say. And we never worried. We
always believed that.

(translated by Bill Brow; NY: Random House, 1983)

Questions

Circle the letter of the answer you think is correct.

10. The three children who died were

a. the narrator's children.

b. the narrator's brothers and sisters.

c. the narrator's nieces and nephews.

d. children in the narrator's village.

11. The passage suggests that the three children
died because

a. of food poisoning.

b. no one took proper care of them.

c. their father killed them.

d. they were too poor to afford proper nutrition
and medicine.

12. The narrator uses which point of view?

a. first-person

b. second-person

c. third-person

d. none of the above

13. The narrator's second paragraph is very short. Why?

   a. She wants to make it stand out.

   b. Because that's all she knows about the topic.

   c. Because she doesn't think it's important.

   d. Because she doesn't like to talk about it.

14. The narrator's family probably lives

   a. in a large city.

   b. in a small town.

   c. in the country.

   d. on a mountain.

15. Many of the narrator's sentences are very short, especially in the last paragraph. Why?

   a. to keep the reader's interest

   b. to show that she hasn't had much education

   c. that's how she was taught to write

   d. all of the above

16. The tone of this passage is best described as

   a. informative.

   b. ironic.

   c. angry.

   d. sad.

17. The tone of the last paragraph suggests that

   a. the narrator doesn't believe what the priests say anymore.

   b. the narrator misses the children who died.

   c. the narrator is very religious.

   d. the narrator doesn't believe in God.

18. The narrator uses the word "died" five times as well as the word "killed" once in this short passage. She does this because

   a. she wants to show that dying is a part of life.

   b. she has a limited vocabulary.

   c. she wants to emphasize how difficult the family's life is.

   d. she is obsessed with the children who died.

CONGRATULATIONS !

You've finished 20 lessons and your reading skills should be much better now. But reading skills are like muscles: If you don't use them, you might lose them. Practice what you learned in this book. Read, read, read! Find some authors that you enjoy. (There's a list of suggested authors and books in the Appendix.) And reward yourself for a job well done!

ANSWERS

EXERCISE 1

1. c. The narrator tells us in the first paragraph that she and Andy "usually take diametrically opposite positions. If I say day, you can count on Andy to say night." (If you don't know what *diametrically* means, you should be able to determine its meaning from context.) The rest of the story shows how they have completely opposite views. Answer (d) is incorrect because Amy tells us that she "love[s] him like a brother." It is true that neither convinces the other (a) and that they're both stubborn (b), but neither of these are the reasons they fight.

2. a. This is the best choice because the story is told by Amy, who is describing a personal experience. Choice (b) is incorrect because the story is in the present; it is not an historical event, and it is not told in the third person . The fact that the selection reveals a conflict (c) does not make the selection a personal narrative. The fact that the selection involves a policy decision that will affect the students (d) does not make the selection a personal narrative.

3. c. This is the best choice because it accurately states Andy's position on the issue of a school dress code. Choice (a) is incorrect because nothing in the narrative suggests that how students dress reflects their parents' views. Choice (b) is incorrect because it reflects Amy's views about the dress code, not Andy's. Choice (d) is incorrect because it does not reflect Andy's reasons for objecting to a dress code.

4. d. This statement is made by Amy to Andy. It does not offer a logical reason to support the dress code. Instead, it tries to make Andy feel insecure about his position by making him feel insecure about himself. The other statements (a–c) are presented as facts and not meant to persuade.

5. a. Support for this answer is found in the fourth paragraph, where Amy describes her own observations and experiences and how they influenced her decision. Her conclusions are logical based on those observations and experiences. Choice (b) is incorrect because nowhere in the story does someone in authority tell Amy to vote, and her explanation does not rely on emotional appeals. Amy does not like designer-labeled clothes, so choice (c) is incorrect. Amy has real reasons for her opinion; it is not based on opposing her brother's views, which rules out choice (d).

6. d. At the end of the story, the reader does not know what the vote will be or what the principal will do, so we cannot effectively predict the outcome.

7. d. The best clue to the meaning is that Andy "can't believe" that Amy "would be willing to give up [her] all-American teenage birthright" to dress the way she pleases. He may be angry (a), but this passage tells us that he also is horrified. Choice (b) is incorrect because he does not deny Amy's opinion; he argues with it directly, which also rules out choice (c).

8. a. This story is told in chronological order, from the PTA proposal to a day or so after the vote but before the announcement.

9. b. Though Amy uses ridicule to make her point (an emotional appeal), she does have a good point to make: that we shouldn't let our clothes determine how we feel. She tells Andy she feels sorry for him because his ego "would be completely destroyed" if he had to wear a uniform. In other words, she's upset that he'd let a uniform affect his sense of self.

EXERCISE 2

10. b. The narrator tells us in the third paragraph that "there were fourteen of us—I and my folks and eleven brothers—even after three children had died."

11. d. The details in the passage suggest that everyone in the family has to work very hard just to get by ("My brothers used to kill themselves chopping and hoeing"). There's no suggestion of wealth or comfort, and there's a sense of helplessness about the deaths. This comes across in the lines, "once diarrhea begins there's no salvation." However, it's reasonable to assume that there could have been salvation if the family had had the money to pay for medicine. In addition, it would be unlikely that a child would become dehydrated if he or she had proper nutrition. There's no evidence to suggest that the children contracted food poisoning (a), and the narrator tells us that she and her mother "would take care of the house," which suggests that they also take care of the little children, so choice (b) is incorrect. Paragraph 3 also describes how the father tried to save the sick children, so choice (c) is also incorrect.

12. a. This story uses the first-person *I* to tell the story.

13. a. A short paragraph like this has the important effect of standing out for readers, so answer (c) is incorrect. Certainly she knows a lot about the topic, since she took tortillas to her brothers in the cornfields, so (b) is incorrect. It is possible that she doesn't like to talk about it, but this is not the best answer because the entire passage deals with difficult and sad issues, so (d) is also incorrect.

14. c. This is the best conclusion to draw based on the evidence in the passage. Her family works in the cornfields, so we can conclude that they don't live in a large city (a) or even in a small town (b). These choices are also incorrect because they seem to have a lack of medical care, which would be more readily available in a city or town. Choice (d) is incorrect because there's no mention of mountains or valleys, and cornfields are not likely to be located in a mountainous area.

15. b. Writers use many strategies to keep a reader's attention, but short sentences isn't usually one of them. Short, simple sentences like these are a good sign that the narrator has a limited education. She tells us that she only went as far as first grade, so she's not likely to be able to write long, sophisticated sentences. Likewise, she uses simple, elementary-level vocabulary words. Choice (c) is incorrect because she probably wouldn't have reached this level of writing in the first grade.

16. d. The word choice in the passage as well as its subject matter create a very sad tone.

17. a. The passage suggests that she doesn't believe the priests anymore. She doesn't say that she doesn't believe in God anymore (d), but she does say that "That's what the priests used to say" and "We always believed that." Ending on this note suggests that they no longer have faith in what the priests used to tell them. She never says that she misses the children who died (b)—in fact, these children may have died before she was even born. Choice (c) is also incorrect because there's no evidence in the passage that she is very religious, only that she believed children went to heaven.

18. c. It is true that she has a limited vocabulary (b), but that is not why she repeats "died" several times. Death is indeed part of life, but this story is about *her* life and her family's life, so choice (a) is not the best answer. There is no evidence that she is obsessed with the children who died (**d**). She does spend some time describing the manner of their deaths, but the description is matter-of-fact and does not make us feel that she misses the children. Rather, this tone makes us see the harsh reality of their lives.

If You Missed:	Then Study:
Question 1	Lesson 1, 4
Question 2	Lesson 11
Question 3	Lesson 16
Question 4	Lesson 18
Question 5	Lesson 16
Question 6	Lesson 17
Question 7	Lesson 3
Question 8	Lesson 6
Question 9	Lesson 16
Question 10	Lesson 1, 4
Question 11	Lesson 19
Question 12	Lesson 11
Question 13	Lesson 13, 16, 19
Question 14	Lesson 1, 19
Question 15	Lesson 13, 19
Question 16	Lesson 14, 19
Question 17	Lesson 14, 19
Question 18	Lesson 12, 19

POST-TEST

Congratulations! You've finished all of the lessons in this book and have dramatically improved your reading comprehension skills. This post-test will give you a chance to measure your new level of reading success.

The questions on this test are different from the pretest, but the format is the same. Take the test, using as much time as you need. Then grade yourself and compare your score with your pretest score. If you have a much better score, congratulations—you've significantly improved your reading comprehension skills. If your score is only a little better, there are probably some lessons you should review. Is there a pattern to the types of questions you got wrong? Do they all seem to deal with the same reading comprehension strategies? Did you remember to read every passage actively?

There's an answer sheet to use on the next page, or you can simply circle the correct answers. If you don't own this book, write the numbers 1–40 on a piece of paper and record your answers there. When you finish, check your answers against the key in the back of the book. The key tells you which lesson covers the skills tested in each question.

Good luck!

1. ⓐ ⓑ ⓒ ⓓ
2. ⓐ ⓑ ⓒ ⓓ
3. ⓐ ⓑ ⓒ ⓓ
4. ⓐ ⓑ ⓒ ⓓ
5. ⓐ ⓑ ⓒ ⓓ
6. ⓐ ⓑ ⓒ ⓓ
7. ⓐ ⓑ ⓒ ⓓ
8. ⓐ ⓑ ⓒ ⓓ
9. ⓐ ⓑ ⓒ ⓓ
10. ⓐ ⓑ ⓒ ⓓ
11. ⓐ ⓑ ⓒ ⓓ
12. ⓐ ⓑ ⓒ ⓓ
13. ⓐ ⓑ ⓒ ⓓ
14. ⓐ ⓑ ⓒ ⓓ
15. ⓐ ⓑ ⓒ ⓓ

16. ⓐ ⓑ ⓒ ⓓ
17. ⓐ ⓑ ⓒ ⓓ
18. ⓐ ⓑ ⓒ ⓓ
19. ⓐ ⓑ ⓒ ⓓ
20. ⓐ ⓑ ⓒ ⓓ
21. ⓐ ⓑ ⓒ ⓓ
22. ⓐ ⓑ ⓒ ⓓ
23. ⓐ ⓑ ⓒ ⓓ
24. ⓐ ⓑ ⓒ ⓓ
25. ⓐ ⓑ ⓒ ⓓ
26. ⓐ ⓑ ⓒ ⓓ
27. ⓐ ⓑ ⓒ ⓓ
28. ⓐ ⓑ ⓒ ⓓ
29. ⓐ ⓑ ⓒ ⓓ
30. ⓐ ⓑ ⓒ ⓓ

31. ⓐ ⓑ ⓒ ⓓ
32. ⓐ ⓑ ⓒ ⓓ
33. ⓐ ⓑ ⓒ ⓓ
34. ⓐ ⓑ ⓒ ⓓ
35. ⓐ ⓑ ⓒ ⓓ
36. ⓐ ⓑ ⓒ ⓓ
37. ⓐ ⓑ ⓒ ⓓ
38. ⓐ ⓑ ⓒ ⓓ
39. ⓐ ⓑ ⓒ ⓓ
40. ⓐ ⓑ ⓒ ⓓ

Directions: Read each passage below carefully and actively and answer the questions that follow each passage. Take as much time as you need for this test. Then use the answer key at the end of the test to check your answers.

IMPROVED LITERACY

Over the past 20 years, worldwide illiteracy rates have consistently declined. The main reason for this decline is the sharp increase in the literacy rates of young women, which is the result of campaigns to increase educational opportunities for girls. For example, between 1970 and 1990, the literacy rate among women in the United Arab Emirates increased from 7% to 76%.

Questions

1. This passage is mainly about
   a. the cause of illiteracy among women.
   b. the effects of illiteracy among women.
   c. the cause of reduced illiteracy rates among women.
   d. the effect of educational opportunities for girls.

2. According to the passage, which of the following is directly responsible for the sharp increase in literacy rates for young women?
   a. the United Arab Emirates
   b. increased funding for education
   c. a drop in illiteracy rates worldwide
   d. campaigns to increase educational opportunities for girls

THE APE CAVES

You will need to know the following words as you read the story:

pumice: a type of lava that is very light in weight
stalactites: icicle-shaped formations on a cave's ceiling

Mount St. Helens erupted with the force of a nuclear explosion on May 18, 1980. Volcanic ash shot 14 miles into the air and fell over the entire Pacific Northwest, from Eugene, Oregon, to Seattle, Washington, and beyond.

I could have safely watched the cataclysm a mere four miles away, from the entrance to the Ape Caves in what is now Mount St. Helens National Volcanic Monument, but the force of the blast would have made the top of the mountain simply disappear.

In fact, the explosion sent ash in the opposite direction from the caves, and later eruptions lightly dusted the cave's area with pumice. At that point, I might have sought refuge in the underground Ape Caves, or lava tube, below. At nearly two-and-a-half miles long, this is the longest such tube in the Western Hemisphere.

The Ape Caves were formed about 2,000 years ago, but they were not discovered until 1951. Early explorations of the caves were made by a local Boy Scout troop, which named themselves the "Mount St. Helens Apes."

Standing in that same location recently, I felt the wind whistle past me, into the cool depths of the cave. My hiking group had chosen to hike the lower part of the Ape Caves first. Most casual visitors prefer this section. It has a downward slope with a sandy floor. Its highlight is the "meatball," a huge, round ball of lava wedged ten feet above the cave floor. Beyond it, the cave ends in a low series of crawlways.

As we descended 40 feet below ground by stairs, the change of environment was striking—from the warmth, greenery, and birdcalls above, to the cool, dark silence below. Sound seemed to be swallowed up by the volcanic walls, and the temperature dropped to a cool and damp 42°. The darkness was so jet black that the beams of our flashlights seemed weak and outmatched by the inescapable inkiness.

Old lava flows had left a variety of markings in their passage. Large gas bubbles had popped at the surface of the molten flows, leaving circular rings, frozen ripples, and deep gutters in the hardened lava on the floor. This made walking an unusual task. On the ceiling, which rose as high as 20 feet in places, small stalactites pointed their mineral deposits down at us from above.

There's a rumor that a local jogger has carefully paced out the Lower Cave and, in doing so, has developed a mental map that allows him to run the route without the aid of a lantern or flashlight. How disturbing it would be for a few cave explorers like us to hear quickly advancing footsteps and then see a jogger appear out of nowhere, run past, and then disappear once more.

After lunch, we elected to try the Upper Cave. This cave is twice the length of the Lower Cave and a much more challenging climb—not a good choice for the timid or unskilled underground adventurer. In the Upper Cave, when our conversation ceased, only the drip, drip, drip of seeping water and our breathing could be heard. Our flashlights soon became an obstacle. There were spots where we needed both hands for climbing over the increasingly large and jagged rockfalls. Where were some miners' helmets when we needed them?

We met two other groups that had turned back after encountering a nine-foot wall of stone in a narrow passageway. The daunting, smooth stone face rose before us. It had once been a dramatic lava waterfall. Refusing to turn back, we boosted one person up over the top. This person got to the next level and then turned to assist the rest of us. Dirty, scraped, and unstoppable, we pressed on.

Just about then, my flashlight went dead. (The guidebook had suggested that we carry three sources of light per person but that had seemed overly cautious.) I found myself fervently wishing for an old-fashioned lantern, or even a book of matches. Our passage slowed to a crawl as we picked our way carefully through the gloom, relying on the beams of our companions' flashlights, anxious not to suffer a fall or twisted ankle.

Fortunately, we were near the exit, close to the end of the Upper Cave. Our tired party had readied itself to climb the ladder into the blinding light when we thought we heard hurried footsteps rushing toward us. Perhaps it was just cave anxiety, but we flew up the rungs in an orderly panic.

Looking back down into dimness, we saw a man walk past in brisk, measured strides, keeping track of something on his digital watch. He wore a sweat suit and carried a tiny flashlight. Looking up, he gave us a quick nod and was quickly swallowed by the dark. We looked up then, too, and blinked in wonder at the dazzling south view of Mt. Saint Helens.

Questions

3. Read the first two paragraphs of the passage again. Then think about this sentence from the second paragraph.

I could have safely watched the <u>cataclysm</u> a mere four miles away, from the entrance to the Ape Caves in what is now Mount St. Helens National Volcanic Monument.

As it is used in this article, what does the word *cataclysm* mean?

a. a creative and dramatic performance

b. a sudden, violent change in the earth

c. a new discovery about the earth

d. an exploration of new territory

4. The author probably wrote this article to

a. encourage people to explore the Ape Caves.

b. inform people about volcanoes.

c. inform people about the Ape Caves.

d. persuade people to visit Mount St. Helens.

5. Read this sentence from the article.

Our flashlights soon became an obstacle.

Based on this sentence, the writer believes that the flashlights are an obstacle because

a. their batteries wear out quickly, leaving everyone in darkness.

b. it is easier to explore the cave with a lantern than with a flashlight.

c. flashlights are heavy and add to the weight that the hikers must carry.

d. it is harder to climb rocks with only one free hand.

6. How do the members of the hiking group get beyond the wall of stone?

a. by boosting one member at a time up to the next level

b. by crawling over the stalactites one at a time

c. by pressing on the stone wall with all their strength

d. by finding a route that goes around the wall of stone

7. The author suggests that the Upper Cave is best explored by someone who

a. is young and quick.

b. has had previous experience as a jogger.

c. has had previous experience as a rock climber.

d. has patience and confidence.

8. Based on the article, which of the following statements about the Ape Caves is **false**?

a. They were explored by a Boy Scout troop.

b. They were formed about 2,000 years ago.

c. They were discovered about 50 years ago.

d. They were buried by the 1980 eruption of Mount St. Helens.

9. Which of the following sentences from the passage expresses an opinion?

a. Mount St. Helens erupted with the force of a nuclear explosion on May 18, 1980.

b. At nearly two-and-a-half miles long, this is the longest such tube in the Western Hemisphere.

c. This cave is twice the length of the Lower Cave and a much more challenging climb— not a good choice for the timid or unskilled underground adventurer.

d. On the ceiling, which rose as high as 20 feet in places, small stalactites pointed their mineral deposits down at us from above.

10. The style of this passage is best described as
   a. distant and matter-of-fact, providing only essential information to readers.
   b. very detailed, using description to create a picture of what it's like inside the cave.
   c. full of short, choppy sentences that create a sense of excitement.
   d. dry and repetitive, with little variation in sentence structure.

TREATING BURNS

There are three different kinds of burns: first degree, second degree, and third degree. Each type of burn requires a different type of medical treatment.

The least serious burn is the first-degree burn. This burn causes the skin to turn red but does not cause blistering. A mild sunburn is a good example of a first-degree burn, and, like a mild sunburn, first-degree burns generally do not require medical treatment other than a gentle cooling of the burned skin with ice or cold tap water.

Second-degree burns, on the other hand, do cause blistering of the skin and should be treated immediately. These burns should be immersed in warm water and then wrapped in a sterile dressing or bandage. (Do not apply butter or grease to these burns. Despite the old wives' tale, butter does not help burns heal and actually increases the chances of infection.) If a second-degree burn covers a large part of the body, then the victim should be taken to the hospital immediately for medical care.

Third-degree burns are those that char the skin and turn it black or burn so deeply that the skin shows white. These burns usually result from direct contact with flames and have a great chance of becoming infected. All third-degree burn victims should receive immediate hospital care. Burns should not be immersed in water, and charred clothing should not be removed from the victim as it may also remove the skin. If possible, a sterile dressing or bandage should be applied to burns before the victim is transported to the hospital.

Questions

11. The main idea of this passage is best expressed in which sentence?
   a. Third-degree burns are very serious.
   b. There are three different kinds of burns.
   c. Some burns require medical treatment.
   d. Each type of burn requires a different type of treatment.

12. This passage uses which of the following patterns of organization?
   a. cause and effect, comparison and contrast, and order of importance
   b. cause and effect, chronology, and order of importance
   c. comparison and contrast only
   d. cause and effect and comparison and contrast only

13. A mild sunburn should be treated by
   a. removing charred clothing.
   b. immersing it in warm water and wrapping it in a sterile bandage.
   c. getting immediate medical attention.
   d. gently cooling the burned skin with cool water.

14. This passage uses the third-person point of view because
   a. the author wants to create a personal and friendly tone.
   b. the author wants to present important information objectively.
   c. the author wants to put readers in his or her shoes.
   d. the author does not have a specific audience.

SYLVIA

For perhaps the tenth time since the clock struck two, Sylvia crosses to the front-facing window of her apartment, pulls back the blue curtain, and looks down at the street. People hurry along the sidewalk. Although she watches for several long moments, she sees no one enter her building.

She walks back to the center of the high-ceilinged living room, where she stands frowning and twisting a silver bracelet around and around on her wrist. She is an attractive young woman with a narrow, delicate face and light brown hair held back by a barrette. She is restless now, because she is being kept waiting. It is nearly two-thirty, and a woman named Lola Parrish was to come at two o'clock to look at the apartment.

She considers leaving a note and going out. The woman is late, and besides, Sylvia is certain that Lola Parrish will not be a suitable person with whom to share the apartment. On the phone she had sounded too old. However, the moment for saying the apartment was no longer available slipped past, and Sylvia found herself agreeing to the two o'clock appointment. If she leaves now, as she has a perfect right to do, she can avoid the awkwardness of turning the woman away.

Looking past the blue curtain, however, she sees the sky is not clear but veiled by a white haze, and the air is still. She knows that the haze, the stillness, and the heat are conditions that often precede a summer thunderstorm—one of the electrical storms that have terrified her since she was a child. If a storm comes, she wants to be at home in her own place.

She walks back to the center of the room, aware now that the idea of sharing the apartment, which was never appealing, has actually begun to alarm her. Still, she knows she will have to become accustomed to the notion, because her savings are nearly <u>exhausted</u>. She has a low-paying job, and, although she has considered seeking another (perhaps something connected with music—in her childhood she had played the flute and people had said she was gifted), she finds she has no energy to do that.

Besides, although her job pays poorly, it suits her. She is a typist in a natural history museum with an office on the top floor. The man for whom she works allows Sylvia to have the office to herself, and from the big window to her left, she can look out on a peaceful, park setting.

Questions

15. Which of the following adjectives best describes Sylvia's mood as depicted in the story?
a. anxious
b. angry
c. meditative
d. serene

16. Based on the tone of the passage and the description of Sylvia at this moment, which of the following is the most likely reason Sylvia's job "suits her"?
a. Her office is tastefully decorated.
b. She likes her employer at the museum.
c. She is musical and enjoys listening to the birds sing.
d. She is able to work alone in a space that feels open.

17. When Sylvia looks out her apartment window, the weather appears
a. gloomy.
b. ominous.
c. spring-like.
d. inviting.

18. Based on the story, which of the following would most likely describe Sylvia's behavior in relationship to other people?
a. distant
b. overbearing
c. dependent
d. malicious

19. Which of the following images is most appropriate for describing Sylvia's state of mind as she waits for Lola?
a. a child eagerly digging for buried treasure
b. a dog joyfully rolling on its back in fresh, green grass
c. a rat trapped in a maze
d. a forest fire

20. The word "exhausted," underlined in paragraph 5, most nearly means
a. tired.
b. weakened.
c. spent.
d. sick.

21. The description of Sylvia's physical appearance in paragraph 2 might be said to foreshadow the rest of the story because
a. silver jewelry suggests wealth and self-confidence.
b. her youth and attractiveness make her perfect.
c. her delicate appearance reflects her shy, reserved personality.
d. the frown indicated tragic plot developments.

22. What is the best word to describe Sylvia in paragraph 3?
a. timid
b. curious
c. irritated
d. sad

ON TOP OF THE WORLD

For over a hundred years, the highest mountains in South America have lured climbers from all over the world. But until 1908, Peru's Mount Huascaran resisted the efforts of all those who attempted to climb to its summit. One mountaineer, Annie Smith Peck, vowed to overcome the obstacles to be the first to the top of Mount Huascaran. In order to succeed, she would have to organize expeditions, deal with reluctant companions, survive bad weather, and climb steep cliffs of ice and rock.

A Love of the Mountains

Annie Smith Peck was born in the United States in 1850. Although she didn't start mountain climbing until she was in her thirties, it soon became clear that she had found her life's work. She started by climbing mountains in North America and Europe. Even as she began setting records, Peck was always searching for the next great challenge. At that time, mountain climbing was not considered appropriate for women, so Peck's activities made her notorious.

The Beginning of the Quest

Peck traveled to Bolivia in 1903 to make an attempt to reach the summit of Mount Sorata. This was her first trip to South America and also the beginning of her lifelong interest in the continent. Her first try at Sorata failed, and in 1904, when a second expedition also failed, she turned her eyes to Mount Huascaran. Huascaran had three features that made it irresistible to Peck: It was a tall peak, no one had yet climbed it, and it was in South America.

Again and Again

Annie Peck mounted four expeditions and made five attempts before she finally conquered Mount Huascaran. All of her failed attempts fell short because of bad weather and trouble with other members of the climbing team. Between expeditions, Peck returned to the United States to raise money. She received help from many scientific organizations, including the Museum of Natural History, which even lent her the snowsuit worn by Admiral Peary on his trip to the North Pole. Still, Peck struggled at least as much to raise money as she did to climb her beloved mountains.

Success at Last

In 1908, Peck scraped together the funds for yet another expedition to Mount Huascaran. This time, she hired two Swiss guides to assist her with the climb. On their first trip up the mountain's slopes, one of the guides became ill, and the entire team was forced to turn back even though they were very close to the top. Being so close to success was very frustrating. Peck could not even prove how close they had come because she had accidentally brought the wrong kind of film and was not able to photograph the climb.

The team rested for a few days, and the guide recovered. On August 28th, they set off again. The climb was extremely difficult. Steps had to be hacked one by one into the steep ice. Snow bridges and crevasses had to be carefully crossed. The weather was so cold that everyone suffered from frostbite. When Peck and her two guides were a short distance from the top, they stopped to determine the exact height of the mountain. One of the guides took advantage of Peck's distraction to climb the few remaining feet to the summit so that he could boast that he had been there before her. Although Peck was understandably angry, she focused on the triumph of achieving her goal. On September 2, 1908, Annie Peck finally stood at the top of Mt. Huascaran.

Life after Mount Huascaran

Peck was 58 when she climbed Mt. Huascaran, but she wasn't done with mountain climbing. Several years later, she returned to Peru to climb Mount Coropuna. At the summit, she left a banner that read, Votes for Women. For the rest of her life, Peck lectured and wrote about women's rights, her expeditions, and life in South America.

Questions

Read the following questions. Circle the answer you think is correct.

23. As it is used in the first sentence of the passage, the word *lured* most nearly means
  a. trained.
  b. attracted. ✓
  c. irritated.
  d. brought comfort to.

24. Which of these events happened first?
  a. Peck planted a banner reading "Votes for Women."
  b. Peck borrowed Peary's snowsuit. ✓
  c. Peck climbed to the top of Mount Huascaran.
  d. Peck hired two Swiss guides.

25. According to the passage, Peck wanted to reach the summit of Mount Huascaran because
  a. the government of Peru encouraged her to do it.
  b. the Swiss guides had dared her to do it.
  c. she was being paid to climb it.
  d. no one else had been able to do it. ✓

26. Information in the passage suggests that on her expeditions to Mount Huascaran, Peck brought along
  a. binoculars.
  b. a camera. ✓
  c. a flashlight.
  d. a map.

27. Based on information in the passage, the reader can conclude that Peck
  a. enjoyed raising money for her trips to South America.
  b. liked South America more than the United States.
  c. enjoyed taking risks and facing challenges. ✓
  d. worked at the Museum of Natural History.

28. The passage suggests that several scientific organizations in the United States probably thought Peck
  a. was foolish.
  b. needed advice.
  c. deserved support. ✓
  d. wanted attention.

29. Which of following best states the main idea of this passage?
   a. Peck had climbed mountains on other continents, but the mountains of South America were taller.
   b. Peck was a popular writer and speaker who climbed mountains in South America.
   c. Peck raised money from many sources to finance her expeditions to Mount Huarascan.
   d. Peck showed much determination in becoming the first woman to climb Mount Huarascan. ✓

30. The main purpose of the information under the *Success at Last* heading is to
   a. describe the obstacles that Peck faced before she reached her goal. ✓
   b. show that Peck suffered permanent physical damage when she climbed Mount Huascaran.
   c. explain why Peck was angry with one of her Swiss guides.
   d. explain why the climb to the top of Mount Huascaran was so expensive.

31. As she is presented in the passage, Annie Peck can be described by all of the following words except
   a. timid. ✓
   b. determined.
   c. purposeful.
   d. adventurous.

A Narrow Fellow in the Grass
by Emily Dickinson

1   A narrow Fellow in the Grass
2   Occasionally rides—
3   You may have met him—did you not
4   His notice sudden is—
5   The grass divides as with a comb—
6   A spotted shaft is seen—
7   And then it closes at your feet
8   And opens further on—

9   He likes a Boggy Acre—
10 A floor too cool for corn—
11 Yet when a Boy, and Barefoot—
12 I more than once at Noon
13 Have passed, I thought, a Whip-lash
14 Unbraiding in the Sun
15 When, stooping to secure it
16 It wrinkled, and was gone

17 Several of Nature's People
18 I know and they know me—
19 I feel for them a transport
20 Of cordiality—
21 But never met this Fellow
22 Attended, alone
23 Without a tighter breathing
24 And Zero at the Bone

Questions

32. Who or what is the "Fellow" in this poem?
  a. a whip-lash
  b. a snake
  c. a gust of wind
  d. a boy

33. The phrase "Nature's People" means
  a. nature lovers.
  b. children.
  c. animals.
  d. neighbors.

34. The speaker of this poem is most likely
  a. an adult man.
  b. an adult woman.
  c. a young boy.
  d. Emily Dickinson, the poet.

35. The phrase "Without a tighter breathing/And Zero at the Bone" suggests a feeling of
   a. cold.
   b. grief.
   c. awe.
   d. fright.

36. The setting of this poem is most likely
   a. a big city.
   b. a rural area.
   c. a desert.
   d. a snowy mountainside.

37. This poem is a good example of which of the following?
   a. logical appeals
   b. the first-person point of view
   c. chronological order
   d. a chain of cause and effect

38. Lines 17–20 suggest that the speaker of the poem
   a. dislikes all animals.
   b. works in a zoo.
   c. has lots of pets at home.
   d. gets along well with most animals.

39. "The grass divides as with a comb" (line 5) is an example of which of the following?
   a. simile
   b. metaphor
   c. alliteration
   d. personification

40. The speaker uses repetition of the *s* sound in lines 4 ("His notice sudden is") and 6 ("A spotted shaft is seen") to
   a. create a soft, soothing sound.
   b. suggest that he has a stutter.
   c. suggest the slithering, hissing sound of a snake.
   d. create a tongue twister for the reader.

ANSWERS

If you missed any of the questions, you can find help with that kind of question in the lesson(s) shown to the right of the answer.

Question	Answer	Lesson(s)	Question	Answer	Lesson(s)
1	c	2	21	c	14, 19
2	d	1, 9	22	c	12, 13, 14
3	b	3	23	b	3
4	c	16	24	b	1, 6
5	d	1, 4	25	d	1, 4
6	a	1, 4	26	b	1, 17
7	c	1, 4	27	c	16
8	d	1, 12	28	c	1, 4
9	c	4	29	d	2, 16
10	b	13	30	a	2, 16
11	d	2	31	a	1, 12
12	a	7, 8, 9	32	b	12, 19
13	d	1, 4	33	c	12, 19
14	b	11	34	a	11, 19
15	a	12, 14	35	d	12, 19
16	d	14	36	b	19
17	b	13, 14	37	b	6, 9, 11, 18
18	a	19	38	d	12, 19
19	c	13, 19	39	a	13, 19
20	a	3	40	c	13, 19

A·P·P·E·N·D·I·X

SUGGESTED READING FOR 8TH GRADERS

This book wouldn't be complete without a list of great books and magazines to read. Studying reading comprehension and answering reading test questions is fine, but the best way to improve your reading ability is *to read.* Read every day, even if you read only for 15 minutes. What follows is a list of books, arranged by category, and a list of magazines. Read what you like, and if you find a favorite subject or author, stick with it. You will be on your way to reading success!

AUTOBIOGRAPHY

All I Really Need to Know I Learned in Kindergarten
　by Robert Fulghum (Ivy, 1993)
Anne Frank: The Diary of a Young Girl by Anne Frank (Bantam, 1993)
Black Boy by Richard Wright (Harper Perennial, 1998)
I Know Why the Caged Bird Sings by Maya Angelou (Bantam, 1983)

FICTION

A Separate Peace by John Knowles (Bantam, 1985)
A Sudden Silence by Eve Bunting (Fawcett, 1991)
After the Rain by Norma Mazer (Flare, 1997)
Bury Me Deep by Christopher Pike (Archway, 1991)
Don't Look Behind You by Lois Duncan (Laurel Leaf, 1990)
Ethan Frome by Edith Wharton (Signet Classic, 2000)
Gentlehands by M.E. Kerr (HarperTrophy, 1989, 1990)

Here's to You, Rachel Robinson (Laurel Leaf, 1995); *Tiger Eyes* (Laurel Leaf, 1982) by Judy Blume

Hoops by Walter Myers (Laurel Leaf, 1983)

Jacob Have I Loved by Katherine Paterson (HarperTrophy, 1990)

Murder on the Orient Express by Agatha Christie (Harper, 1991)

Nectar in a Sieve by Kamala Markandaya (Penguin, 1998)

Ordinary People by Judith Guest (Penguin, 1993)

Runner by Cynthia Voight (Fawcett, 1986)

The Arm of the Starfish (Laurel Leaf, 1980); *A Wrinkle in Time* (Yearling, 1973) by Madeleine L'Engle

The Call of the Wild by Jack London (Tor, 1990)

The Catcher in the Rye by J. D. Salinger (Little, Brown, 1991)

The Chocolate War (Laurel Leaf, 1991); *We All Fall Down* (Laurel Leaf, 1993) by Robert Cormier

The House on Mango Street by Sandra Cisneros (Vintage, 1991)

The Human Comedy by William Saroyan (Dell, 1991)

The Kidnapping of Christina Lattimore by Joan Lowery Nixon (Laurel Leaf, 1992)

The Language of Goldfish by Zibby O'Neal (Puffin, 1990)

The Moves Make the Man by Bruce Brooks (HarperTrophy, 1996)

The Outsiders by S. E. Hinton (Puffin, 1997)

The Pearl by John Steinbeck (Penguin, 2000)

The Pigman by Paul Zindel (Bantam Starfire, 1983)

Things Fall Apart by Chinua Achebe (Anchor, 1994)

To Kill a Mockingbird by Harper Lee (Warner, 1998)

Violet and Claire by Francesca Lia Block (HarperCollins, 1998)

Where the Red Fern Grows by Wilson Rawls (Bantam, 1984)

PLAYS

A Raisin in the Sun by Lorraine Hansberry (Vintage, 1994)

Romeo and Juliet by William Shakespeare (Oxford, 2001)

SCIENCE FICTION/FANTASY

A Wizard of Earthsea by Ursula Le Guin (Bantam Spectra, 1984)

Animal Farm by George Orwell (Signet, 1996)

Child of the Owl by Lawrence Yep (HarperTrophy, 1990)

Dragonsong by Anne McCaffrey (Bantam Spectra, 1977)

Fahrenheit 451 by Ray Bradbury (Ballantine, 1995)

Flowers for Algernon by Daniel Keyes (Skylark, 1984)

Hanging Out with Cici by Francine Pascal (Pocket, 1978)

Life, the Universe and Everything by Douglas Adams (Ballantine, 1995)

Remembering the Good Times by Richard Peck (Laurel Leaf, 1986)

Robot Dreams by Isaac Asimov (Ace, 1994)

The Blue Sword by Robin McKinley (Ace, 1991)

The Hobbit, Lord of the Rings by J. R. R. Tolkien (Houghton Mifflin, 1999)

The Lion, the Witch and the Wardrobe by C. S. Lewis (HarperCollins, 2000)

The Old Man and the Sea by Ernest Hemingway
(Scribner, 1999)

The Red Badge of Courage by Stephen Crane
(Tor, 1997)

Watership Down by Richard Adams (Avon,
1978)

MAGAZINES

Boys' Life
This is a great general interest magazine for
boys. Read about a wide variety of topics.

Creative Kids
Appropriately named, this magazine is meant
to encourage your creativity.

Cricket
This is a general interest magazine with stories, recipes, science articles, and games.

Dig
Want to be an archaeologist? *Dig* is a perfect
magazine for you. Mummies, dinosaurs, and
ancient civilizations fill its pages.

Explore!
This magazine sets out to answer the question "How does the world work?" There are
plenty of adventure, science, and technology
stories from all over the world.

Girls' Life
This magazine has plenty of advice, stories,
celebrity interviews, and other topics of
interest to girls.

Kids Wall Street News
Show me the money! This magazine is a great
introduction to saving, investing, and learning about the economy.

National Geographic World
With great articles about wildlife and world
cultures, this award-winning magazine is
perfect for pleasure reading.

Sports Illustrated for Kids
Are you a sports fan? Check out this magazine and read all about your favorite teams,
players, and sports events!

Teen Voices
A great magazine written by and for teen girls
that focuses on real-life topics.

Time for Kids
From the editors of *Time* comes this current
events magazine filled with great articles,
photos, and maps.